A HEALTH INSPECTOR'S MEMOIRS

STEPHEN V. SCHULTZ

authorHOUSE

AuthorHouse™
1663 Liberty Drive
Bloomington, IN 47403
www.authorhouse.com
Phone: 833-262-8899

Published by AuthorHouse 04/28/2023

ISBN: 979-8-8230-0581-4 (sc)
ISBN: 979-8-8230-0582-1 (e)

Library of Congress Control Number: 2023906720

Print information available on the last page.

Any people depicted in stock imagery provided by Getty Images are models, and such images are being used for illustrative purposes only.
Certain stock imagery © Getty Images.

This book is printed on acid-free paper.

This book is dedicated with Love and appreciation to my lovely wife Krystyna, for her gracious and compassionate caring for me over 33 years of marriage.

CONTENTS

ACKNOWLEDGMENTS

I wish to thank all those individuals who supported my career in serving the public. I always tried to help the industry while working as an inspector for 24 years.

Thank you for the cover illustration! Graphics by artist Ray Flores. His effort and devotion to his art was greatly appreciated and added to the right touch for the book.

INTRODUCTION

The past had been a clear future ahead of me as I had spent time in the military and remember going with my warrant officer to the line battery kitchens to inspect their mess halls. The warrant office was a character that thought he knew everything but really relied on me as a specialist first class to make all the decisions and write everything down. Then he would go back to the headquarters and take all the credit for the work we did together. Most of the time it was to make sure the black spots in the mashed potatoes were not the mess sergeants tobacco from his stub cigar he always held in his mouth. I think they all used to read <u>Beatle Bailey</u> in The Stars and Strips and tried to look like the mess sergeants depicted in the cartoons.

Anyway, after finishing college I found myself in public lodging running an apartment complex to put a roof over my wife's head. We rented units, cleaned them between occupants and found that we could paint them for just under $500.00 and save a little for ourselves. The funniest experience was the three a.m. call I got from a tenant that heard a terrible racket coming from her ceiling fan in the bathroom. I told her it could wait till morning and she insisted I come right now. Long story short it was a bird that had made his way down the vent from the roof and I fell off the ladder as it escaped into the apartment.

The worst experience was the evening around 4 p.m. and there was such a party going on in our pool area just in front of our apartment at the center of the complex. I looked out the office window and noticed all the people did not live at our complex and no one had any bathing suits or clothes on their bodies. First, I grabbed the phone and called the local police and then told my wife that I was going to the pool to treat it with acid for the evening. She warned me but I was young and full of assurance that I could clear them off the property before the police got there.

I opened the locked gate that they had all climbed over hanging their clothes on the fence that surrounded the pool and I headed for the pump shed telling them they had better get out of the pool as I had to add acid to the water. When I did this they all came scrambling out of the water. They all spoke Spanish and all I could understand was they were not happy. I then proceeded to lock the gate again and this big moose of a Spaniard came to me and decked me with a sucker punch. I awoke looking up at the town police helicopter as a dozen or more police cruisers were surrounding the pool. The call must have reached every police officer in town that there was a nude party going on at the apartment complex. I learned what a stupid mistake it was and I had a shiner to show for it.

Then I moved on to break another cardinal rule in life: never work for a relative. My wife and I hired in to work for her uncle, running an American plan resort. The offer included a two-story house to live in as general manager. We were to hire that staff, which were mostly returning college students; two from each state in the union, to work as waiters, waitresses, and also help entertain the guests. The resort sat on a 16-acre plot of land bordered by a wine vineyard, a river, and grazing lands for the horses. The activities included horse back riding shows, volleyball, tennis, basketball, two swimming pools, bonfires, boating, canoeing, and a dance hall for square dancing and bingo. The food was prepared and served family style in a very large dining hall where families or groups would sit together. The first night of dining consisted of T-bone steak, com on the cob, beans, salads, and ice cream for dessert. The steaks had to bc cooked on a grill by the general manager. Great fan fare was celebrated, as I had to present each steak to the table as lots of ooze and ahs from the hungry guests around the tables.

The experience was wonderful but ended on a sour note as the relative drove into the driveway after the first season was over and told us to get a U-haul and get out. He had sold the property in less than one year and he only bought it for an investment. He was driving a brand new car and looked like he had just won the lottery.

So we went back home and I started working for the company that I used to cruise through the driveway when I was a teenager. Mostly hotdogs, hamburgers, and fish and chips were on the menu. The work was steady but boring and I stayed long enough to earn some vacation time and we went to Florida. It was there while on vacation, I answered an ad for a Howard Johnson's manager. To my surprise they hired me immediately, offering to pay all our moving expenses and to start next month.

My first experience in Florida was short as the company used me in eleven months to manage eleven different properties to determine why they were losing money. At one restaurant I hired in as a dishwasher one day and showed up the next day to let everyone know that I was sent by corporate as his or her manager but was told to send everyone home because they were fired for stealing product and cash from the restaurant. The last Ho Jo's I managed was doing quite well and then I received a phone call asking me to return to Michigan.

It was an offer to be the general manager of a 24-hour truck stop on 1-75 in the middle of the state. Again, they offered to move my family and I was to start next month. Back in Michigan we started in April and we got the worst snowfall that shut the place down for four days. We were giving the food away and allowing people stranded to stay in the restaurant as well. I was asking myself, why did I leave Florida.

The one lesson I learned while working at the restaurant was service was the cheapest advertisement. One day a lady customer screamed and called for the manager. I promptly approached her and she stated that her waitress had poured hot tea allover her dress. I saw the waitress shaking her head and I asked the lady if she would mind wearing a waitress uniform while I had her dress cleaned at our dry cleaners next door. She hesitated and then said she would. So, half hour later I brought her dress to her and asked her if it was O.K. She was delighted and went to change after she had finished her lunch. She came out of the restroom and asked for her check. I told her, "Madam, there is no check. But, please come again."

She was shocked and said she had to tell everyone how she was treated. Later, I told the waitress, she was the shift head waitress, that I thanked her for not arguing with the customer. We all knew that our policy was to allow the customer pour their tea. It was the cheapest advertisement I could have purchased.

During the next five years I spent running the restaurant, I encountered several health inspectors. They came on like gangbusters in the beginning. Later when they knew we were serious about public health and attacked all the problems they would address on their inspections we came to a mutual understanding. They usually left with a compliment on how well we maintained the establishment for it being a 24-hour restaurant.

At the end of five years, I was ready for a change. I moved five miles to the north and helped open another new truck stop. I wanted to go back to Florida and decided it was time. Back in Florida, I applied for a health department job with a county health department. The job included everything from day care centers, schools, water bottling plants, and restaurants. The restaurants were to be inspected prior to the State of Florida Department of Hotels and Restaurants coming in to license the establishments.

I liked the job the State was doing and legislation was ongoing to turn the inspection of Hotels and Restaurants over to the State employees and leave the counties out of the program in order to get a better uniformity. It was then that I applied for an opening with the Department of Business and Professional Regulations. They hired me and I became an official State Inspector with the Division of Hotels and Restaurants. Finally, I had found a home.

Most of my fellow employees where older individuals from varying backgrounds such as retired business owners, veterans, and not to many fresh college graduates like I had found in county government. My boss was an old timer that had a gift for handling his workers and staff so that they shared respect for each other. He was always helpful and patient as long as you accomplished the goal of his district. The goal was to complete your entire list of accounts with their required number of inspections for the entire year.

This goal was easily achieved as long as you were not a slacker and you didn't get hung up on one account for to long. We had enforcement with a hearing officer that would not listen to any excuses from people brought to hearings. Fines were levied and violations corrected and everyone was satisfied.

Now, I will begin to tell you about the Memoirs.

CHAPTER 1

OUR MEETING

It was a hot, sultry South Florida day as I pulled into my little gray house I had rented for the last two years. It was a nice little bungalow, just two bedrooms with a bath but the rent was what I could afford. It was my escape from Lakeworth, Florida, where the crime had become un-bearable. They actually tried to steal my Eldorado Cadillac right from my front yard. Therefore, it didn't take me long to find this nice little place in Stuart, just 20 miles North in Martin County. Aside from the place not having air conditioning and an occasional palmetto bug, it was the best move I ever made. Little did I realize this was the beginning of a whole new life

My white Ford station wagon, a Florida State owned vehicle, while working as a health inspector, had just made the turn into the driveway and my neighbor came running over to greet me. She was a Portuguese-Brazilian lady, short, big busted, and full of energy that ran a furniture upholstery business out of her back door. She was always calling on me to help her move furniture or fix something around her house. She was a good person but always taking advantage of an opportunity as she found herself divorced and single. She never knew that I was divorced also. So, I was sure I was going to be asked to do something even though I was hot and tired from looking at dirty restaurants or busy hotels, all in a days work.

Surprisingly, she said in her slight accent, "Steve, come over here right now! I want you to meet my new house guest".

Just then, I noticed a women coming around from behind my neighbors house pushing a lawn mower that sometimes was self propelled but mostly ran like it was on its last wheels. The women wore white shorts, a white blouse with embroidery on the front, and a pair of shoes, which had a solid heal from the toe to the back. She had bright golden blonde hair, slightly curled, but starting to mat from the heat of the afternoon and from the effort she had to put into pushing that old lawn mower.

I glanced at her and thought to myself, here is my neighbor taking advantage of an opportunity to get her grass cut. My neighbor explained, "Steve, come to the back yard with me. I want to introduce you to my guest. She is from Poland". I still remember to this day, replying, "Oh, that's right, I heard a good Polish joke today!"

When I looked back the lawnmower was gone from the front yard and had gone around to the back. As my neighbor and I walked up her driveway to the back yard, I noticed a few people sitting outside in yard chairs. We exchanged introductions and then my neighbor called the girl over that was running the lawnmower. Reluctantly, she turned off the mower, and tried to straighten her hair and wipe her forehead all at the same time.

I could immediately tell this is not what this girl was used to doing but was quite capable.

"This is Krystyna. She is from Poland. Krystyna, this is Stephen Schultz, he is my neighbor from next door," said my Portuguese-Brazilian friend. I reached out with my hand to take hers as a jester of greeting. I could tell she was quite embarrassed. Her palm was sweaty but gentle and I knew from the start that this girl was more refined than her present condition had placed her. I said something simple like it is a pleasure to meet you. She responded with a nod of her head as she looked down and said, "Nice to meet you to, as she turned to go back to her work she had begun, cutting grass. My neighbor said, "No, no, come and have some ice water with us". Krystyna, waived her hand in the air and said, "Later after I'm done here".

This, I would later find to be Krystyna's nature. She never stopped until the job was done and she was determined to finish first, any job she had started before anything got in her way. She was the most energetic individual I had ever met and never sat still for longer than a minute. She had a drive in her to be successful and not let anything get in her way of accomplishing her goals. I was struck, immediately, that this girl I had to get to know better.

I excused myself, and went back to my home to fix a hot dog with chips. That sounds about right, as I had been single now for eight years after a divorce. I usually, stopped for a hamburger or something like that so I wouldn't have to fix something for just myself at home. It was terrible eating alone but was necessary. My son Brian would come to spend the weekend and then we cooked something for us that would be more substantial.

It must have been a Friday, because the very next day I was watching a late college football game (one of my passions in life), when I noticed Krystyna, walking slowly past my house on the sidewalk across the street. I was in a recliner and enjoying a fierce battle between two rival university football teams. It was amazing but there I was getting out of that recliner and going to the door to see if for sure it was Krystyna. And as quick as a wink I was across the street and stopped this lovely lady. I remember the line I used on her, as I was not a very smooth conversationalist, but it worked.

"You shouldn't walk alone in this neighborhood," I said. This was an outright lie but an affective approach to a beautiful girl that didn't know where she was.

We walked very slowly and I tried to get Krystyna to talk about herself. I could tell she was quite unsure of her English and that she was trying to remember a lot of words that she had learned. You know the standard greetings they teach you if you are traveling or just cordial phrases that she was doing very well at for the short time she was here in this country.

The wedding turned out to be all I had expected but later in my marriage I learned that our wedding was nothing like a Polish wedding. The church ceremony was adequate in that we had the difficulty with the Catholic Church so we settled on the Lutheran church. The guests were few but honored to be there and we cherished having them attend. We made a video of the proceedings and only regretted the Ava Maria was not on the tape. Our reception was held at a Knights of Columbus hall and we enjoyed the music and dancing. Everyone danced and I found out that Danuta was everything Krystyna had told me about her. She loved to dance and was always the first one on the dance floor and the last one to leave. She had so much energy it was impossible to keep up with her.

Krystyna and I decided not to take a honeymoon and postpone the occasion for a trip to Poland later on in the year. Unfortunately, we were to find ourselves on other trips we had not dreamed could happen.

The first month of Danuta's visit to the United States was settling into a routine of working during the day for the Jones as a Nanny and later in the evenings, spending time at our little house. We welcomed her company and Krystyna was able to make her feel at home by speaking Polish to her. We would all go outside and walk around the neighborhood. This is when Danuta would try to teach me some Polish.

It started with stepping out with our left (lewo) foot and then our right (prawo) foot and to go straight ahead (prosto), Repeating this over and over again as we walked, I finally got in my head to stay. Also, one evening Danuta came to our house with a car that was on empty and she stayed so late it was hard to find a gas station open in our sleepy little town. As she drove down the street, I was in the passenger side telling her lewo, prawo, or prosto until we finally found an open station.

Danuta was quickly picking up on English as well. She and well as Krystyna would write new words down repeatedly until they thought they could remember them. Krystyna was exceptionally well at this and she would pass it on to her sister. I was always marveling at the progress they were making and the lack of progress I was achieving in the Polish language.

Our days were pretty much spent apart as I had a job with the State of Florida and Krystyna and Danuta were keeping the children busy as well as taking care of the home where Danuta was staying. They also had time to visit with their relative, Uncle Frank Wilk, who invited Krystyna to the United States. They really enjoyed visiting with each other and Frank was quite good at learning more and more of the Polish language.

CHAPTER 2

GREETINGS

The procedures for a state health inspector entering a business establishment were well documented in the regulations, we had to study the first couple of weeks into the job. It was also wise to review and be tested on the procedures throughout the career of a health inspector.

It never amazed me by the number of experiences an inspector would be confronted with and the ability to handle each and every one of the events properly and sometimes improperly as the years passed.

One of the first chuckles I would get is when I entered a restaurant establishment and they would recognize me either by the clipboard the inspector would carry or the recognition of seeing me there before. Sometimes, it could be honest shock, sometimes horror, and sometimes a friendly glad to see you.

The first greeting: "OH MY GOD!" by the employee would be responded by me immediately replying, "No, I'm your state health inspector. Could you please let your owner or manager know that I am here and would like to see him?"

The second greeting: "JESUS CHRIST!" by the employee would be responded by the same introduction. It was nice to see that these employees had such a good Christian understanding of the leaders of their faith but to take their names in vain like this told me they were not to religious. And I knew that I was probably in for a long inspection that day.

A restaurant that was ready for their inspector would usually greet you with a welcome and we have a few questions to ask of you. They would also immediately contact the person in charge to let them know that you had arrived. These were the best relationships and you were prepared for a good inspection with little if any problems.

Then there were the oriental restaurants that greeted you with the invitation to sit down and enjoy a meal before you start your inspection. This must have been a custom in their old country or the way they ran their home. The official must be full before he can do his job or if he were full he wouldn't write so many violations. I can still here the familiar greeting: "YOU COME, YOU EAT!" The response was always the same, "No thank you, can you get the person in charge please?"

Now, the public lodging industry had a bit of a different greeting experience. The state regulated and inspected hotels, motels, bed and breakfast, rooming houses, and apartment building with five or more units on a single property. The inventory was vast and you had to really be efficient to complete the assigned number of establishments. The state departments goal was always 100% completion.

Hotels were always a time consuming adventure. First, the front desk staff had to notify the management that you were there. Depending on the size of the establishment, either a single manager would go with the inspector or if it were a five star hotel an entire management staff would escort you around the property. The contrast would always set the experience of what kind of inspection was to follow.

The one five star hotel I enjoyed inspecting would send the assistant hotel manager (usually a striking good looking and very efficient woman), head of housekeeping, building maintenance director, and grounds keeping manager. The restaurant food and beverage manager and chef would join after the lodging inspection was completed. The time was spent while waiting for this staff to come together, inspecting licenses, booking registry, and required notices to be posted at the front desk for guests.

All of the managers carried in house phones to notify staff members of violations noted on the inspection report and the immediate attention given to the correction of these shortcomings. I was always impressed with their professionalism and their attentiveness to detail. I knew I was dealing with a five start rated establishment. I really liked going through the property from the catacombs in the basement, to the power plant, to the laundry, and then to the executive suites and the average room. The inspections of the rooms entailed ripping the linens from the bed and looking at every crook and cranny in the room to make sure it was spotless.

Then there was this one hotel that had a very large property, which included not only a hotel, but condos and time-share resorts as well. Almost all the time I introduced myself to the desk staff and that I needed to see a manager, they all looked at each other like they were in another world. Later, I realized that there was such a turnover in management, desk staff, and generally everyone on the resort staff that they didn't know what to do. I finally just went to the head secretary on the resort that had been there since the first corner stone was set and she notified the proper people to go with me. The property wanted to be a five-star but was never able to claim more than four. Unfortunately, it was all very much miss managed.

The motel inspection started with a greeting by a manager or owner at the front desk. It was usually a mostly friendly atmosphere and a very cooperative adventure. They knew what was expected of them and had most everything in order. Only on occasion did there have to be confrontations when a property changed ownership and the state was not notified and a new license had to be registered. The greetings were surprised and the owners were not prepared for the requirements they did not know about.

The apartment inspections left me with two experiences I can never forget. The first was in the beautiful town of Palm Beach. The streets were always lined with glorious vegetation of immaculately trimmed hedges, palm trees, and cut grass. The air was always full of the aroma of freshly manicured lawns. This particular day, I was very new on the job and was quite proud of the responsibilities I was given to inspect these quaint apartments that populated the little town.

Approaching the stoned driveway it was quite apparent the only vehicle in the parking area was a shiny Rolls Royce. The year I could not distinguish as they all looked alike to me. I went around to the back and noticed an open door at the top of a wooden fire escape. The stairs looked like they needed paint and had two levels before reaching the top. Proudly I stepped on the first set of stairs and reached the first landing. There I heard a loud crack and found myself supporting my upper body with my arms spread and my hand clutching the clipboard. My legs were dangling about two foot off the ground.

There appeared a head out of the doorway at the top of the fire escape it yelled, "Who are you? What are you doing there?"

I yelled back, "I'm your state inspector! I presume that is your Rolls Royce out front there?"

His response was, "Yes it is. I'm so sorry, let me come down there and help you up!

I didn't realize the stairs were in that bad a shape."

No harm was done to my body but the fire escape was later to be replaced by a newly constructed egress approved by the town fire marshal and myself. I was later to find out that the owner of the property was an uncle of the famous stage and movie family Barrymore. Mr. Barrymore had a home here in Palm Beach and a home in La Jolla. His Rolls Royce collection numbered over thirty.

Later a meeting was set to meet at Mr. Barrymore's home with the town fire marshal. A plan was approved of the new fire escape and the construction was to be completed within the week. I received my first bribe as an inspector, which was my choice of a Rolls Royce to drive home. I said I could not and the town fire marshal said, "Thanks and I'll return it in the morning, Mr. Barrymore." Later in my years as the inspector of Mr. Barrymore's property I was to learn that Mr. Barrymore was killed in one of his Rolls Royce cars in La Jolla, California.

My second greeting I will never forget was during an inspection of an apartment complex. It was a two story newly constructed complex with balcony entrances on the first and second floor. Just as I was rounding the corner of one of the front buildings that faced the street but was also surrounded by vegetation I came upon a startling sight. She was lying on a large beach towel, back side up, and all I could say was, "Oh!" Then I lied and said, "I'm sorry."

The young girl, who was possibly in her twenties just got up, grabbed her towel and not even covering up said, "That's all right. I was going in now anyway!"

No violation that I could see but I had a hard time removing the ink mark that I had just ran across the inspection report.

CHAPTER 3

THE MERCEDES

Early on in my career as a health inspector on the county level there came a time when I was eager to volunteer for a mission I will always remember. It happened on a Thanksgiving weekend when a terrible storm crossed the Atlantic and swept a Venezuelan cargo ship named the Mercedes on the shore of Palm Beach. It would not have been such a big deal except the ship landed on the neighbor's beach next to the Kennedy Estate. This ship hit the shoreline so hard that it cracked the neighbor's swimming pool.

Now the ship's crew had abandoned the ship before it came ashore. By the time the ship was in the exclusive town of Palm Beach there were only ship rats on board. The health department determined that the rats would stay on board as long as there was food available to keep them alive. Therefore the director of the health department ordered all the food removed from the ship and asked for any volunteers to accomplish the mission.

A young co-worker and I decided it would be quite an adventure and a break from out usual routine of inspecting restaurants, schools, daycare center, and rooming houses. So we were chosen and preceded to survey the location.

The only access to the beach was a gated path next to the distressed neighbor with the cracked swimming pool. Many people had gathered outside the gate and around the driveway of the estate, which included the local media with all their equipment and TV cameras. We tried to avoid all the publicity hounds and entered the gated pathway after showing our ID's from the health department.

We first noticed people you trying to get as close to the stranded ship as possible and were really causing quite a nuisance. They were discussing how they were going to board the old rusty bucket of bolds and rivets. We started to make notes on what we felt needed to be done to control the site and what we would need to go aboard and accomplish what we volunteered to do.

We reported back to the health department and planned our next visit the following day. The health department came up with some bright orange suits that looked like contamination equipment, hoods and all. So off we went with our suits and hefty garbage bags to save the ship from their hungry rats.

We first decided to post signs on stacks all around the base of the ship. The signs read: DANGER – KEEP OUT - by order of the HEALTH DEPARTMENT. We were also required to post to the same signs on the side of the ship. This was a problem that we were not prepared to address on this trip, as we had no means of climbing up on the sides of the vessel.

We looked very official, as we were getting into our orange suits complete with boots and gloves. The helmets were put on as soon as we got aboard by throwing a gaff hook and rope to the railing on the side of the ship. First my partner climbed the rope hand over hand keeping a grip with his rubber boots on the side of the ship. Once on board, I started to throw the garbage bag boxes to him and then the flashlights. Now it was my turn and I was surprised on how agile I was to getting on board so easily.

Now we found ourselves in a very scary situation, as there was not a sound on board and no lights inside the ship. As we made our way down into the lower decks to find the galley we were always expecting a ship rat to scurry across our feet or over our heads. We did not feel like heroes or explorers but just scavengers.

Sure enough, there was all this corn meal and grain lying around on the counter tops, shelves, and in boxes. We found a couple of large burlap bags full of some kind of grain on the floor. We proceeded to throw the food into the garbage bags as fast as we could while trying to hold the flashlights for each other. We had about a dozen garbage bags full and decided to first throw them overboard and come back for the two burlap bags. To our surprise a crowd had gathered along the beach to watch our every move.

After the burlap bags landed on top of the other garbage bags on the beach we went back aboard one more time. We felt pretty sure we got all the food and decided to do a little exploring. We found the captains quarters and that he had left his uniform behind hanging on a hook by the port window. I looked around on the floor and found a large square box with a combination on its top. I picked up the metal box and something went clunk inside it. I thought maybe a gun or ship log. Anyway, we left these things behind and felt better about it because it was not our assignment.

We went back to the health department and threw all the bags into a dumpster. We decided the next day we should post signs on the side of the ship, so we called the local fire department for assistance with a ladder. The next day we climbed the ladders and posted our signs with good old duct tape from bow to stern on the shore side of the Mercedes.

Later we were to hear on the local news of all the articles that was salvaged from the ship during the night by all the local divers. They had boarded the ship from the ocean side and they were doing it all legally. It would not have mattered if we posted signs on the ocean side.

It took several months for a salvage company to be contracted and through much pulling by tugboats and drenching the old Mercedes left Palm Beach. Its final resting place was to be scuttled for a reef off the coast. I remember calling my uncle up in Michigan, to come down to Florida and I could get him a real old classic Mercedes. All he had to do is haul it up north. He didn't come.

CHAPTER 4

LIFE SAVING EVENTS

How ironic just as I am writing this book that a couple that owned a local motel greeted me in our local Walgreen drug store. They asked if I heard that the mother had passed away recently and the father and daughter had just gotten the motel back in their hands. It had been sold about two years ago to a very unsavory operator and he never paid them any money other than the original down payment.

We stood there in the store talking about how I liked retirement and then the subject came up about the life saving event that happened many years ago at their motel. It was quite a reminder and gave me the feeling that all those years inspecting did mean something in that particular incident.

I had just finished checking all the smoke detectors in the twenty units they had on the property and found unit number four to have a dead battery. This was before the laws changed and smoke detectors had to also have an electrical line backup. So the owner ran back to the office and got a new nine-volt battery and installed it into the smoke detector. The detector was located in the hallway just in front of the bedroom door and just down the hallway to the door leading to a carport.

This small violation that was noted and comments added that the violation was corrected passed the owner and I as just a routine inspection event. We spoke for a while about how the business had been this season and then I departed to continue my scheduled route.

As the events occurred is second hand from the fire department personnel and the owner of the property. It seems that a construction worker who had rented number four that evening invited a guest to join him for the evening. They must have been out very late, got back to the unit, went to bed. Then the construction worker picked up by a fellow worker around three in the morning. The construction worker had parked his big pickup in unit number four's carport and the engine was running very hot.

At about four in the morning sirens rang out and smoke and flames engulfed the pickup, carport, and had burned the doorway exit. By the time the flames had reached the bedroom doorway the smoke detector finally went off. The young lady who was a guest was quickly awakened and she looked for the quickest way out. Climbing through the only window in the room she ran to the end of the unit that was not burning

When she turned the corner of the unit to run toward the center street that divided the property she was greeted by a very surprised young fireman. The girl was wearing only her birthday suit and long blonde hair.

She was frightened, cold, and grateful that they were there to help her. A second fireman brought a special blanket for her and all was well. The fire was contained in a short time.

When the story made the morning news I just had to stop at the motel to look at the damage and speak to the owner. We both commented on how fortunate the smoke detector had the battery installed the previous day and the lady was able to escape the burning unit. I felt very blessed to have done my job and a life was saved.

Not all events found such immediate resolutions but in one case I was glad that I was inspecting a resort hotel that was just newly constructed and open for business. Being the thorough inspector I always prided myself in being, I would go to every maintenance room in the building. This particular survey found me opening the door to the air conditioner cooler towers on the top floor.

To my amazement there was a maintenance man walking out on two by four wood pieces stretched across concrete walls on either side of the cooling towers. He was trying to perform some mechanical work with wrenches as he stood on the two by four on his tiptoes as high as he could reach. I called to him and asked why he was working under these conditions without a scaffold.

He stopped working and came to the concrete wall side to explain. It seems there were contract disagreements between the owner of the hotel and that general contractor. So, the contractor did not complete erecting the catwalk that was to be erected around the towers. This I felt was an unacceptable situation for the safety of the workers.

It took one telephone call to a federal agency I had never contacted before but felt it was the right thing to do. OSHA was called and they sent someone out immediately. Within two days the catwalk grates were in place and the maintenance crew thanked me.

Unfortunately, OSHA found a list of other things that they wanted completed that week also. One of the items was a palm tree required by landscaping codes that was planted after the opening inspection. It stood in front of a fire exit door that could not be opened without hitting the tree. Go figure!

CHAPTER 5

HAND SINKS

If you were to ask someone: What is the most important piece of equipment in a restaurant? What do you think they would answer? Would it be a grill, refrigerator, freezer, deep fryer, electric slicer, or dishwashing machine? I would bet the last thing they would think of is a hand sink.

During a plan review before the kitchen plans are approved special attention is given to the location of hand sinks. Their proximity to the workstation in question is always considered. The cook must have the hand sink close to his prep area where he can reach to wash his hands between tasks that prevent cross contamination. The number of hand sinks are also determined by the size of the kitchen and if two or three are placed throughout the work place all the better. Even near the kitchen door to the front service area so waitress and staff can clean their hands after handling soiled surfaces. The dish washing area is also required to have a hand sink so the staff can wash their hands between handling dirty dishes and clean dishes.

More food borne illnesses are caused by lack of hand washing than many other sources of contamination. It is therefore the inspector's responsibility to enter a food prep area and immediately wash his hands properly making sure there is hot water available, proper soap, sanitizer, and disposable towels.

One inspection at a local pizza parlor I noticed the establishment had but one hand sink in a rather small food prep area next to their three compartment sink. The hand sink was a porcelain fixture with the proper valves and spout but was unfortunately broken on the corner and only two thirds of the sink was usable. The owner did not feel there was a problem because they would always use the three-compartment sink when necessary. Even if the sink was full of dirty pizza trays or pots and pans.

I explained under no circumstances are three-compartment sinks to be used as hand washing facilities. They have not always been left sanitized and therefore could not assure the user that his hands became sanitized as well as there was no soap dispenser or paper towels near the three-compartment sink. The owner stated that they would use a wiping cloth towel to dry their hands. Wrong!

The violation was sited and the establishment was given two weeks to comply. Upon entering the restaurant at the grace period given the owner said, "Wait till you see what we accomplished since you were here last!

"Wonderful!" I replied, "Can I come back and see what you have done?"

When I went behind the front counter and headed to the hand sink, the owner said, "Don't you notice anything different?"

"Yes, I see you have a new hand sink," I replied as I approached the sink that was the object of my return visit.

The owner says, "No, don't you notice the new floor we put in?"

I then turned the hot water valve on the hand sink and said, "Oh, yes it is nice."

The owner screamed, "Oh, don't turn the water on. We haven't had time to put the plumbing under it since we were so busy with the new floor."

The water spewed all over the place getting my shoes and the nice new floor wet. I reached to turn the water off and just looked at the owner in disbelief. I said, "Are you serious?"

The hearing was short and to the point. The owner paid the $1000.00 dollar fine and looked forward to my follow-up inspection to see the fine helped to correct the hand sink.

Many times at different establishments the inspector would find the hand sink sometimes used to hold dirty utensils, pots, rags, and just about anything except dirty hands.

One bartender would always use the hand sink to store his tips from his labor at the bar. Each time I would tell him that it is not to be used for his personal bank but for him to use it to wash his hands. He explained to me that he washes his hands only when he goes to the bathroom. I asked him, "Then you never wash them after emptying dirty condiment bowls or dirty dishes left on the bar by his clientele.

'Well, I would wipe my hands on my bar towel," he tried to explain.

This guy needs to go back to bartenders school is what I wrote on the report and gave them the violation. At the next inspection, again he was using the sink for his tips and he was shocked when I drowned them with a full force of water until it became hot.

There ensured a very disgruntled rage from the bartender as the manager came out of the kitchen. He knew the past history of the bartender's unwillingness to change his bad habits. The violation was corrected on the spot and no further use of the sink for tip collection was noted. If he washed his hands in the sink is still a question to this day. Maybe he will go to the bathroom after each customer.

One of the more prominent and upscale restaurant chains introduced a talking hand sink. It did follow a contamination scare with an employee that had hepatitis C. Anyway it was quite the state of the art invention. It could speak any programmed language; give the management a printed report at the end of the day, listing each employee and how often they washed their hands at that station. It also had a warning alarm that went off if the employee walked passed the hand sink with soiled hands and did not stop to wash them.

CHAPTER 6

CORRECTING VIOLATIONS

Regulations required violations to be corrected by a time specified by the inspector.

The time can be by the next routine inspection, within two weeks, or 30 days. Major violation would have to be completed by a re-inspection anywhere from 24 hours, or whenever the inspector needed the violation corrected. I would always try to work with the owners, as our original program was degreed. That was to work with the industry to protect the public.

Therefore whenever I could get a violation corrected as soon as possible the better. The major violations having priority and the minor violations as soon as possible, they all had to be corrected. Many of the situations were quite easy to accomplish as I drew upon my experiences in the past and tried to help each owner the best I could.

The first request during a restaurant inspection was to see the establishment's license. It was required to be posted on the premises, current, and available for the guests to see.

There was one owner that was a wonderful cook, caterer, and could present a beautiful dining facility. Her greatest shortcoming was the ability to keep her records and paperwork in order. Basically, she could never find her license.

Once when we finally found her license, it was delinquent. We updated the license collecting the fee and left knowing the license would be mailed to her. On the next scheduled inspection the license was not posted and could not be found. After a search of her mail that had accumulated we found the license. I had enough of this continued violation but knew the owner's problem. Her restaurant was small and she was trying to fill all the responsibilities of an owner and would forget the paperwork till the last minute. The customer's meal was the most important.

I took it upon myself to go to the nearest Walgreen drug store, purchased a one-dollar picture frame and a stickem hook. When I returned to the restaurant that day I put the license into the frame and mounted it on the wall next to her cash register. Violation corrected, the owner was very grateful, and the license was always kept up to date and posted in the same frame from that day forward.

We had a hearing program to fine for violations that would not be corrected. The lodging program got to be a bit monotonous when it came to apartment buildings. Most owners are proud of their properties and always want to keep them repaired and clean.

It came about that one property owner wanted to test my patience and I had to bring him into hearing with several violations at several different locations that he was the owner. It was a case of giving the owner so many warnings and violations not being address after writing on the inspection reports, talking on the phone, and a face-to-face confrontation, I finally, resorted to the hearing.

Our hearing officer was a big, strong, strait talking, no nonsense enforcement officer.

The hearing was held at the district office and the inspector was invited to attend. Prior to the hearing the inspector was allowed to bring the enforcement officer up to date on the violations sited and the current status of the violations. It was in this case, I told the enforcement officer, the owner wanted to test our resolve.

The owner entered the hearing office with a bad attitude. He grumbled that this was costing him a very long trip for nothing and he was not going to correct anything the inspector had asked him to do. He also immediately stated that he was one of the highest taxed people in the county and he was able to pay all of his taxes on the properties.

My proudest moment was when my hearing officer told the man to sit down and listen to what he had to say. The inspector had given him able time to correct all of the violations sited on the inspection reports of all seven of his properties. He was happy to hear that the owner was financially able to meet all his tax obligations and therefore he would be able to meet the financial responsibilities that the hearing officer was going to levy on his property.

The owner was quite taken back by the way my hearing officer spoke to him. He settled back in his chair and relaxed. Then the hearing officer started to tally the number of violations and multiply the sum on his calculator next to the file folder holding the stack of cases he was to hear today. The owner of the property was starting to squirm in his seat as the calculator keys started to click faster and faster.

Finally, the hearing officer stated, "Sir, your total fine for your seven properties will be four-thousand five hundred dollars to be paid before you leave or within thirty days. The violations will be completely corrected by the next call back inspection that will take place in two weeks. If they are not corrected you will be seeing me in this same office again. Do we understand each other?"

The owner almost fell out of his chair. He said, "I'll make arrangements for the check to be here within thirty days. The violations will be corrected and good day to you, Sir."

The violations were completed on schedule, the owner never confronted me again, and the money was received as promised.

CHAPTER 7

HOT DOG CARTS

The program for hot dog carts was bounced around from the county health inspection to finally land in the lap of the state health inspection program. It was challenging because there existed such a variety of the units, always changing ownership, and they were mobile and therefore hard to locate.

Finally, the regulation was changed so that every hot dog cart had to have a commissary. Any restaurant or food service facility with an overhang on the back of the building and a can wash would be considered an adequate commissary. Can wash is another topic of discussion that will be mentioned in another chapter.

All hot dog carts are operated with an LP gas to heat the water to boil the hot dogs. The tanks are mounted on the frame of the cart and must have three gas-shut off stations.

One is the valve on the LP tank; a second is a pressure valve that must be mounted properly between the tank valve and the burner valve, which is the third shut off valve. These are to be inspected each time to be sure they are operating properly and safely.

The hot water must be at least 165 degrees to cook the hot dogs and kept at a minimum of 170 degrees after they are cooked. The hot dog cart must also have a three compartment sink which can be three stainless steel containers that will hold the utensils, like a fork, spoon, or tongs. The hand sink may be a fourth compartment or a separate hand sink attached to the side of the hot dog cart with hot and cold water. Drains must be provided for dirty-water from the hand sink.

This is all to be inspected after you have introduced yourself to the hot dog vendor who has produced a valid license for the unit, a food manager's training card, and letter from the commissary they are using to clean and store his cart.

Thus started the inspection of the famous topless hot dog carts. They came about after a few interested business ladies decided to increase the condiments offered to the hot dog eating public throughout the area. The first and most famous operator, we will call her, started on Okeechobee Blvd., in West Palm Beach. There she was creating such a traffic jam, the city decided to make some quick code enforcement changes, that required screen blocking around her establishment.

The price of hot dogs skyrocketed and the lines for her product still got larger. The location finally had to be moved into another area of the city that would accommodate the traffic. The news media didn't help the situation as the customers had to search for their breakfast, lunch, or snack each day as the hot dog cart kept moving further and further West. Finally, with competition the hot dog girls became very numerous in all parts of the county.

The inspectors had a very hard time making it through the crowds to get the hot dog cart inspected. There was much interest in the thorough completion of each inspection and the slightest violation would have to be addressed immediately. The department would be getting calls on both sides of this dilemma and we were just hoping the problem would eventually take care of itself.

One of the most daring of the hot dog girls worked out in the rural area where the sugar cane truck drivers ran their routes. She was so very young, but only wore a bikini and a hula-hoop to while away the time between customers. Unfortunately, there were a lot of tire tracks from braking and U-turns on the road. Later in my career she approached me in a restaurant while my wife and I were dining out one evening. She said, "Mr. Inspector, don't you recognize me?"

I replied, "Were you a waitress or hostess at one of the restaurants I inspected?'

"You remember, me and my hula-hoop out on Indiantown Road!" She laughed.

Eventually, the novelty did wear off and the hot dog carts returned to normal operation.

A good operator with the right location was usually bringing home around five hundred dollars a day.

The most successful operators were two girls that started a hot dog wagon that operated in a busy industrial park area of town. Later just one of the gals worked the wagon and she also owned her own commissary. Her menu was expanded and she was selling sloppy-Joe burgers, tacos, and salads. She is still operating today and I like to stop and see her and ask how she is doing. She also liked that I was her first inspector when they built the business and the only one that treated her properly.

The hot dog cart introduced the BBQ wagon and then the Stainless Steel Mobil Kitchen. The BBQ rigs were pretty popular to a segment of our society and always fought for bragging rights as to the best ribs, sausage, or chicken. It was very scary at times inspecting the BBQ establishments. They were usually manned by just one operator that was busy cooking and they didn't have time to stop cooking, making orders, or pushing out beverages along with collecting the money. The wagons were always borderline sanitation risks. It was difficult to explain anything to the operator while he was working so an inspector would have to get to the location before they opened for business or wait till the evening just before closing. I was glad to hear the one I was having trouble with finally lost his lease on the property where he was due to lack of payment. Problem solved as he went out of business.

The other BBQ wagon had a very longstanding good reputation and survived the neighboring competition. As far as I know the owner is still operating and I see him on television every once in awhile pitching the best BBQ in town.

A very young couple that really did a nice job built the best wagon I had the pleasure of inspecting from the ground up. They were very professional and when I gave them their opening inspection, I was so impressed with their knowledge, preparation, and complete command of their operation. The unit was totally constructed with stainless steel paneling surrounding the kitchen. Across the back wall was reach-in refrigeration units consisting of freezer and cooler space.

Their cooking equipment was all brand new from grills to fryers and a suppression hood system. They were ready to start serving the public as they had a commissary already licensed by the department. Their first client was a retired professional golfer who was very well known in the area. The menu was very high scale serving steak and lobster for the golfers Christmas party, held every year at his residence.

It was an honor and a privilege when it came time to inspect this wagon because I knew it was going to be spotless. It was time for a bit of the good after inspecting some of the bad.

CHAPTER 8

A GIRL NAMED MARIA

You know, every once in awhile you meet someone that really impresses you and earns your respect. Maria is one of these people that I met in the early 80's. She had come from Mexico and was working at a very busy and popular eating establishment. I would frequent the eatery on the weekends and always saw her there working.

I also had the job of inspecting this establishment and the owner was a Greek fellow that had worked hard his entire life. He knew the secret to success was hard work. Greeting the owner at the front of the restaurant is where he always seemed to be. From there he would greet his guests, play hostess, and when there was trouble from the kitchen it was just a short trip to turn around and tend to a problem from the cooks window.

Throughout the many inspections I had at this restaurant, I was always addressing the concrete floor in the food prep area. It had been there from previous owners and was never repaired properly. Maria was in the dishwashing area and would follow me as soon as I entered. The first time I met her; she was washing the dishes by hand in a three-compartment sink.

Maria always had the sink full of dirty pots or pans, trays, or the dirty dishes from the front of the house. The volume of work she had to do was enormous. She never complained and I was constantly telling the owner that the place needed a dishwashing machine. He would agree and say that they are working on it.

Back to the floor and the conditions that always seemed to be needing mopping and sweeping because the floor drains were not located properly so that the water would drain from the floor. Maria would always grab a mop and quickly respond to my complaints about the water and tell me through her broken English that she would take care of it.

The owner was true to his word and soon the establishment had a new dishwashing machine that used hot water for sanitizing. It was always kept clean and operating properly thanks to Maria. She appreciated the machine and always worked very hard to maintain it and keep everything around it clean. Still the floor was a problem with too much water on the floor.

Again, the owner finally started to install a brick floor throughout the food preparation area and the dishwashing area. It seemed to take forever as he was having a Greek friend do the work and each time I visited the place as a customer, the owner had to show me their progress.

Just about the time the establishment was receiving good evaluations on its floor cleanliness in the kitchen, the place was sold to a major restaurant chain. The first thing the operators did was tear up the kitchen floor and put in a nice smooth tile floor.

Maria was out of a job but not for long. I found her working a local eatery not far away and she was cooking. Now, Maria was all of maybe five feet tall and she was behind this pass through window that required her to really stretch and stand on her tip- toes to reach the window. Never one to complain, she took charge of that little kitchen and made sure everything was spic and span.

It was always a pleasure to see her working so hard and smiling from ear to ear. I would enter the kitchen and as I reached for the can opener (always an easy violation to find food on the blade) she would beat me to it and place it in the three-compartment sink. She would say it is being cleaned so it can't be a violation.

We would proceed to the walk-in cooler and she would make sure that everything that was placed in the walk-in was dated and marked. She was so efficient it made me upset because I had to really work to find a violation. If I did she would say it wouldn't happen again and usually it didn't.

The restaurant owner sold the business and I kind of lost track of Maria. I was moved out of the area to inspect in another town and didn't get back to see the new owners or if Maria was working there or not.

Now that I am retired I stop into Maria's American Café as often as I can and am so proud of her as she not only owns one but two cafes. I hear from the new inspectors that they have a very hard time finding any violations in her places because she is always just one step ahead of them. The last I heard they had to find some crumbs under a microwave shelf. Knowing Maria the way I do she got on her tiptoes and whipped the crumbs away as quick as the inspector wrote the violation.

Maria is the essence of what immigration to this country should be all about. Work hard and keep focused on your dream and you will succeed. She did not try to take short cuts, look for government to help her, or expect someone else to give her a handout. She took what was available to her, that being a dishwashers job and never let losing a job stop her until she owner her own business.

CHAPTER 9

BRIBERY

Bribery as defined in Webster Dictionary: bribe: n. 1. gift made for corrupt performance of duty. ---v. 2. give or influence by a bribe.

The department was always concerned about any actions that an inspector would be tempted or offered any such gift or monetary item in the performance of their duty as health inspectors. Most of the individuals hired by the department had to meet certain criteria that included honesty and clean backgrounds. This was very much the norm but there were a few incidents that were brought to light and corrective actions taken.

The usual inspection program would have the inspectors change areas so that a well-known relationship might be interrupted or not allowed to become to friendly between owners and inspectors. One such occasion was given to me at a very prestigious golfing complex, which included several food service facilities as well as a four-star hotel.

I was shocked to hear that the inspector fired and when I began my inspection of the facility they operators asked, "Would I be expecting the same type of gift that the last inspector received?"

I replied, "What do you mean?"

The operator stated that the last inspector was receiving a golf pass for eighteen holes of golf each time he came to the property. That was around one hundred and twenty dollars for one course.

I explained that the inspector is no longer with the department and this kind of conduct is never allowed. We had a firm understanding and unfortunately I found violations that the property should never have gotten away with and they eventually came before our hearing officer.

Another time during a first inspection of a pizza parlor in a larger town I expected to have a simple opening inspection. I introduced myself to the owner and we exchanged some normal conversation. He stated that he had come down from Long Island, N.Y. and had owned a pizza parlor up north. He then reached into his shirt pocket and placed a fifty-dollar bill in my shirt pocket.

I immediately said, "What are you doing? You better take that back right now or there will be no license issued but only a citation for bribing a state health inspector."

His response was one of shock and he tried to explain that this was the way things were done up north where he came from. I explained to him, he was welcome to Florida but that is not the way things are done down here and he was very close to being fined up to one thousand dollars.

He received his license after the opening inspection and I recommending he should read the regulations on restaurants and to keep a copy on hand as required for future reference.

I still see to this day a gentleman that used to own a pizza parlor here in my home- town that had a problem with seating. It seems his establishment was large enough for more seats than he had but because he was in a shopping strip on septic system, the county environmental health department limited his seating to fifty seats.

I would come for the inspection and he would beg me to have more seats. I would explain to him again that my hands were tied and there was nothing he could do. Then he made a statement to me that really made me mad.

He said, "Sir, just let me know what your bank account number is and you can look the other way."

"Where do you think you are, in Italy? You had better not say another word or you are going to be in more trouble that you can imagine. He no longer owns the pizza parlor but each time I see him in the front row at the church, I often think he must be confessing his transgressions. He is always friendly and smiles as he asks me how I am doing.

My last incident of bribery came one day when I went to that Greek restaurant on a day that I was not inspecting there but was working in the area. I had stopped for lunch and had done several motels close by.

Entering the establishment the Greek owner was at his usual spot near the counter and cash register. We exchanged casual talk and I noticed the owners of one of the motels I had inspected were in the dining room off to the side. I sat down between the entrance and the dining room where they were seated.

After lunch, I asked the Greek owner if I might ask a favor of him. I had not opened a checking account in town yet as I had just moved there within the week. Would he please cash my payroll check for me and then I could pay for my meal. He said of course and took my check after I had signed it.

He came back to my table and started counting out the bills on the edge of the table. The owners of the motel came along just as this was occurring. They said rather loudly, "Oh, is this how he stays open?"

We immediately started to explain and I realized how this must have looked. Bad decision on my part and never made that mistake again.

CHAPTER 10

ROACH COACHES

I am not sure how these vehicles got the slang term of roach coach but it probably had to do with seeing one or two of the critters in the many compartments. The vehicle is usually a pickup truck with a unit slid onto the back truck box. It is designed to hold ice, which is filled just prior to leaving the commissary and is emptied every night to be ready for the next morning.

The trucks can be found usually hanging around construction sites, auto service centers, anyway there might be construction or contractor workers around. They are the source of sandwiches, cold drinks, snacks, coffee, and in some instances hot meals. The vehicles are of varying shapes and sizes but generally just serve cold pre-wrapped sandwiches. Metal doors that closed around the sides and back of the box protected all these products.

The coaches sometimes travel long distances from their commissary and therefore start early in the morning preparing their rigs for a full day of service. Sometimes it was difficult to find a vehicle that was operating without commissary and without a license. We would sometimes stop on the road if we saw one that did not have any recognizable markings, like their name on the door or side of the box in the back.

It was best to schedule the number of vehicles to be inspected on an early morning and arrange for them to be at their commissary. While they were reading their vehicles with ice and products the inspector would make sure all the paperwork was in order and then take temperatures of the products and make sure the food being sold was of the best quality.

The operators would pull into a location that they had on a routine route and honk their horn several times to let their clientele know they had arrived. The operators tried very hard to stay on schedule so the client had better know exactly what they wanted and be ready to pay cash. If you were not at the truck when he was ready to leave they very seldom reopened the rigs for you.

This mode of feeding the workers of America probably goes back to the chuck wagons that used to feed the cowboys of the old west. Hot dogs and hot coffee from an urn were on the rigs; and therefore LP gas tanks produced hot water. They also had to have a working hand sink and a disposable container for waste.

The trucks were sometimes privately owners and then many were owned by a single company and leased to the operators. Most of the time the operators were men but the ones that generated the most money were the good looking, fast moving, sweet acting ladies. They would take the time to know their clientele by name and would usually start preparing their meal for them as they set up their rig upon arriving.

It was truly a different industry and a different king of operator but they all tried very hard to make a living and I always respected them for that.

CHAPTER 11

THE FARM

The earliest of days as an inspector we did most of our work with Number 2 pencils and paper inspections forms. It was easy to keep track of our inspection process as we had what was referred to as street cards and a printed computer run off sheet that listed all the locations that had to be inspected. The inspections were to be completed every quarter for food establishments and lodgings except apartment buildings were inspected just twice a year.

The first time around an inspector had to find all the locations and after that they were pretty sure they could find the locations again. I was quite disturbed about a set of cards in my file that was labeled The Farm. It was to have twelve cabins and a restaurant. It was located about in the center of Hobe Sound in Martin County. Finally, after a quick trip from I-95 east on Bridge Road, I pulled into a gravel parking lot on the corner of U.S. 1 and Bridge Road.

As I got out of my vehicle to look around, it seemed to be a very old property as the wood appeared unfinished on the outside of the main building and the cabins that were duplex structures didn't appear to be in any better shape. The shingles were missing in several places, no apparent sign on the property, abandoned gas pumps, and I was wondering if there were ghosts in residence.

One of the gas pumps read ETHYL and my childhood days came back to me as I remember my grandmother name was Ethyl. We would always reply to my dad when he said we needed gas and us kids would yell, let's go get grandma Ethyl. Warily I made my way to the only door on the main building facing U.S. 1. As I swung the door open I was surprised to see what looked like a log cabin restaurant in the State of Michigan.

The walls were actually constructed of pecky-cypress wood, with beams running across the ceiling, ceiling fans hung motionless, and a slight glow came from a room behind a bar that ran three quarters of the way down the length of the room. Out of the room behind the bar came an elderly matronly looking lady carrying a small pot of something hot as I saw the steam rising over her hand.

"Hello" I said, "I am a health inspector here to find a place called The Farm?"

"You've got the right place young man, my name is Mrs. McArthur, but everyone calls me Mom," she said with a bright warming smile.

"Is this place really a restaurant?" I said.

"It used to be, but I am just warming up some soup for one of our old local natives that stops by to join me for some lunch. There isn't much but you are welcome to join us," she replied.

"Are you charging him for the soup?" I asked.

"Heavens no! He is just an old friend and we will share a Pepsi and some old stories," she said.

Just as I was about to ask her some more questions a rusty old gentleman came in the door and strode over to the bar to sit at the first stool nearest the door.

"Howdy, my name is Digger (he used to be a grave digger)." What's yours?" he quickly said as he climbed onto the stool.

"Steve", I replied.

"He is a health inspector," Mom added, "I think he wants to do an inspection."

I peered into the room that looked like it was a kitchen and notice a flame from a burner on a beautiful shiny six-burner stove. Over the stove, it looked like a thirty-inch fan mounted on the outside wall for an exhaust. The floors looked clean but cracked and worn from traffic and not sealed like foodservice floors are supposed to be.

They settled down to eat the hot soup and sip at the cold Pepsi that she brought from a standing refrigerator in the back room. I hated to interrupt them but was content to look around this old place, as it seemed to be more like a museum. The back wall of the bar held memorabilia of past events of the establishment. A picture of a stately man on a poster for a political office was displayed. There were also pictures of children and

I could tell that Mom was in several of these and I therefore assumed they belonged to her.

Mom was so contented to have me look around as she hummed a song from a long time ago and joined her guests as they finished the lunch. She asked me if I had any more questions and I replied just one that I could think of at the moment.

"Do you still hold licenses for the lodging and the restaurant?" I asked.

"Why yes I do," she said, "They send the renewals to me every year and I pay them right on time."

"But the electric lines to the cottages are cut and appear to not be in use. You don't sell anything out of the restaurant, so why do you keep the license?" I asked.

"Well, I suppose that maybe some day my son will return home and want to reopen the place, so I keep the license active." She said smiling a bright grin and a sparkling eye that had my heart hoping her wish would come true.

We talked for quite awhile and the native guest listened in as Mom told me her family had migrated down from Michigan. Her late husband was an Iron Ore boat captain on the Great Lakes. He wanted to retire and move as far away from the lakes as he could to raise his family. The family car broke down in front of The Farm and that is as far south as they got. They had raised their kids here and they are all departed to different parts of the United States. Her son Harry was in California catering the opening of the President

Regan's Library. He was then going to go to Hawaii for a while.

I told her that I had originated from Michigan as well and knew the Great Lakes very well. She was so easy to talk to and so full of stories about The Farm. It seems the history of the place goes back to its grand opening Pear Harbor day. The folks were quite elderly and wanted to move on, so the McArthur's became the owners when their car broke down.

I didn't want to stop talking to her or listening to her stories but I had to get back to work. I let her know that she no longer needed to renew the licenses for the establishment and I probably would not be seeing her again for an inspection. But if she didn't mind, I would love to come and visit her again on my own time. She thanked me and we parted as I made notes in my car to discontinue the license. The Farm was no longer in business.

It was about three months later, I was told, that Mom woke up in the middle of the night grabbing her head and saying, "What was that nice young man's name?"

She had just gotten a call from her son, Harry, and he was coming home and hope he could open the restaurant and the cabins on the property. She was very excited and just knew that her lifelong dream was coming true. Now, if only she could remember where she put that nice young man's business card. The next morning she arose bright and early and found my card stuck behind some other memorabilia at the collage behind the bar.

When I reached for the phone as I got out of bed around seven o'clock that morning, there was this excited voice on the other end. "Mr. Schultz, could you please stop to see me today?" The voice seemed very happy.

"Certainly, I will stop on my way back from down south of you. It will probably be in the late afternoon.

My day was unimpeded and I was happy to get to The Farm earlier than expected. There was Mom sweeping the floor in the dining room as I entered the building. She rested the broom against the bar and came running to meet me at the door.

"He's coming, he's coming home," she was so happy, "Harry, is coming home!"

Now I had to let Mom know about the new requirements for restaurants and gave her a plan review packet. I asked her to give us a call if they had any questions and I would always be available to help them get the establishment operating again. The licenses would be issued upon the completion of the opening inspection.

I left her quite worried about all the new requirements and if her son Harry would be able to meet the financial endeavor before him. It seems Harry was quite successful in his own world out west and he brought a lot of experience and finance with him. He was a very likeable individual with all the warmness of his family background, personality, and friendly smile with a booming voice to greet you.

It is impossible to explain all the difficulties The Farm had to face before it was renamed Harry and The Natives. First and most expensive was the installation of a new exhaust hood with a suppression system. Then Harry insisted on a new ten-burner stove and graciously gave the old six-burner to a neighbor who was opening a sub shop. The neighbor never forgets how generous the McArthur's were to him in his time of need. Believe me, this was only the beginning of this family's philanthropy.

The most contentious improvements came when Harry installed central air conditioning. Mom was very upset as she thought this was frivolous and an unnecessary expense. The Farm had never had air conditioning and there was always a sea breeze to keep everyone cool. Harry had won out, but added an outdoor dining area with a canvas roof.

The outside dining area was complete with an exterior bar, stage, and gift shop that used to be the old gas station building for ETHYL gasoline still out front. The stage was a sign of Harry's need to party. After all he was a single guy and loved the ladies, as they all received back massages, free of charge from Harry when they sat down. The sign on the entrance to the restaurant says it all: SERVICE IS PROVIDED FOR THOSE WEARING SHOES AND PANTS. ANY LADIES NOT WEARING PANTS PLEASE SEE HARRY.

The stage was also later to be used by Doctors and Nurses playing their instrument on a Wednesday night to raise money for children with cancer or some other infliction that they could not afford the hospital bills.

There was always a jar to collect donations for someone in need whether it is for transportation of a cancer patient, or burn patient, or just a family in need due to a fire or other disaster. The McArthur's were always there.

Now Harry had another wild streak in him as he displayed his collection of hats, his 30-caliber machine gun suspended over the bar, or his double headed calf between the doorways to the kitchen. He also had a knack for decorating T-shirt with the wildest saying and selling them on site. The most popular had a map of the United States and the weather was shitty everywhere except at the big star locating Harry and the Native where the weather was sunny.

The only problem Harry had after the original opening inspection and those to follow was a time when a supervisor accompanied me on the inspection. The supervisor was amazed and said he had never seen anything like it. His only complaint was the pecky-cypress panels behind the three-compartment sink had to be sealed. Harry installed a Plexi-glass panel over the pecky-cypress.

The best was yet to come. Harry eventually installed two new bathrooms on the north side of the building. His talented sister Paula beautifully decorated them; with a very large Betty Boo painted over the men's urinal. The bubble over her head stated, Oh, that's the cutest little thing I ever did see!!

They were a beautiful addition and the place was running very smoothly. One Sunday morning my wife and I invited our neighbors to have breakfast at Harry's. The place was packed and there was a waiting line.

Eventually we were seated but had plenty of time to take in all the signs that had to be read and laughed about. Finally, we had gotten our coffee and sent the waitress off with our order. Then all of a sudden here comes Harry and all his cooks and waitress doing a line dance one behind the other through the dining room tables. Harry was wearing a rubber lobster hat and had a fishing pole with a rubber chicken on a loop holding it out in front of him. He said, "I hope all you folks can be patient, as soon as I catch this chicken, we will get your eggs out to you!"

Everyone just started laughing and applauded their enthusiasm and friendliness under such stress. That was Harry for you. Never let the little things get you upset for there is always a happy customer that comes first.

We would have to answer complaints by consumers when it was called into the department. We would do an official inspection and address the complaint and try to determine if the complaint was legitimate or not. One such complaint came to my attention at Harry and the Natives.

It seems there was a customer that complained that the urinals were mounted to tall and he could not use them. He also stated there was dust hanging from the 30-caliber machine gun as well as the hats between the rafters. Harry and I noticed the complaint was valid on the dust and this was to be address that evening by the staff staying late.

Harry told me the complainer had threatened him by saying if Harry gave him one hundred dollars he would not turn in the complaint. I told Harry I would be back in the morning to answer the complaint and hopefully it would be complied.

I showed up on time and immediately notice the dust had been removed from the machine gun and all the hats and memorabilia between the rafters and behind the bar. I had in my hand a wooden stool with flowers painted on the stool that I had laying around my garage. I gave it to Harry and told him to put it in the bathroom for the complaining customer. Harry told me he had spoken to the individual again and he was sure he would never be back in the restaurant.

I completed the report on the complaint, marking it complied and spelled out in detail as to how it was now complied.

Mom is now in her mid 90's; no longer volunteers to sing every Monday, while the restaurant is closed, at the local senior care home. She can still be seen visiting the restaurant usually accompanied by one of her daughters but still remembers that first day I came into The Farm.

The latest charitable and humanitarian project Harry and The Natives have been pursuing is the feeding of wounded warriors and their families on Wednesday nights. They do this through the help of the local Marine reserve units in the area. This is their way of paying back the great sacrifices these warriors have made for us.

I would like to recommend Harry and The Natives if you ever get to Hobe Sound, Florida on the corner of Bridge Road and U. S. 1.

CHAPTER 12

RURAL APARTMENTS

It came about that my area was expanded to an area west toward Lake Okeechobee where I had the experience of observing an entirely different culture and lifestyle. It was a real awakening to me and not one I was used to so eventually I had to ask for help from my leaders in Ft. Lauderdale.

First the town was known as Pahokee and I was to inspect apartment building where the sugar cane workers were living with their families. The area was really overcrowded because it was the sugar cane cutting season. Many times the employees are brought over from the islands and you can never imagine what else they bring with them.

The buildings were usually cement block structures with metal doorframes and sometimes wood or metal doors. The hardware may be in place or will be reinforced with several hasp or additional locks. The bathrooms maybe centrally located and used by several residence when needed.

An inspector had to look for necessary repairs needed, such as, stairwells, railings, and doors off their hinges, bathroom cleanliness and supplied with the proper necessities. Exit lights had to be lit at all times and hand held fire extinguishers in their proper places from the egress of an apartment. Also, the grounds around the building must be kept clean and free of any litter.

This was a constant challenge as all of these things could be violated at one location or at several locations. It came to my attention that all of these buildings belonged to the same landlord. I investigated and found he had an office in the same town of Pahokee on the main street. So, off I went to find the owner and his office, which was located behind this huge glass windowpane advertising Brahma Bull Stud Service.

I entered the office carrying my clipboard and look like the typical city bureaucrat to this redneck huge gentleman that met me with a big handshake and a smile. "How, can I help you?" he hollered.

I introduced myself and told him why I was paying him a visit. He responded by introducing himself as Mr. Tillis. I thought for a moment and asked the question that was on my mind, "Your not the real Mel Tillis?"

"No, but he is my half brother," he replied.

"So, who does the stud service around here?" I said sounding like a real city slicker.

"My Brahma bulls do or anyone else's bull that can do the job," he offered.

So now that was out of the way I explained that I needed to have these violations corrected at the property he owned. I went over with him each and every violation and then got his signature to complete the contract with his assurance that the violations would be corrected with thirty days.

Mr. Tillis was very polite and understood what I wanted. He was not nervous and as a matter of fact asked if I had time for a little story. I said I had some time before I had to leave.

Now he had to tell the story every health inspector was eager to hear. It seems that Mr. Tillis had traveled out to Branson, Missouri to see his half brother's show. Mel Tillis was up on the stage and saw his brother sitting in the chosen seats and let the audience know just that. Mel said that reminds me I have to tell you about the last time I went home to Pahokee. My half-brother was out in the outhouse for the longest time and so I went out there to see what he was up to. He had a fishing pole and was fishing down into the hole in the outhouse. I said to him what in the world are you doing?

He says to me, "Well Mel I dropped my jacket down the hole and I'm trying to get it out."

I says to him, "You wouldn't wear that sticky dirty old jacket now would you?"

"Heck no," my half-brother says to me, "but I got a perfectly good sandwich in the pocket!"

I rolled out the door laughing and looked forward to our next meeting. I hope all the violations would be corrected if he wasn't to busy with his Brahma Bull Stud Service.

Thirty days later I was back in town, inspected Mr. Tillis property and found all the violations I had cited were taken care of to the fullest capacity. He must be good at his stud service business too, I thought.

Unfortunately, on that same trip I inspected a new account and found the most deplorable situation I had feared. One Haitian family was living in a single room apartment with table, chairs, a sofa, ducks, goats, chickens, and a couple of rabbits.

I had a camera with me and took the pictures so no one would think I was trying to embellish the story. The children were very proud of their animals and tried to gather then all together for me as they posed for the pictures.

The owner was not in town and I would have to contact him either by phone or by certified mail. This I accomplished by setting up a meeting to take place the following week between the owner, my supervisor, my director, and myself. The trip back to the rural apartments found the same situation. The only one who was not shocked by the whole event was my director. He said he had seen this kind of thing before and it was resolved by the owner of the apartment building letting the people have another vacant apartment next to their animals. Since this was all on the first floor level it worked out to everyones satisfaction. The only other problem was the litter and debris the animals were creating and the Haitians promised to clean everything.

I thought I had seen everything but this I never expected in working in the rural Okeechobee area.

CHAPTER 13

ROOM 999

There was one motel in my past that I must say will always bring good memories.

When I first inspected the property it gave me quite a scare as there were so many violations and the owner was not really up to the task at hand. It belonged to an elderly couple with the lady doing all the administrational work and the gentleman doing all the outside and inside the room work. The property was unique in that it had its own septic plant that had to be maintained.

The owners had taken over the motel with the best intentions of fixing it up and to resell it as soon as possible. Unfortunately the violations required immediate correction or the motel could not operate. Fire equipment was lacking, smoke detectors not provided, air conditioners not working, plumbing in disrepair, beds without sheet covers or the proper linens, and then there was the sewer plant that they knew nothing about. I knew that a license contractor had to maintain the system as required by county environmental health. The motel also had a swimming pool to be inspected by the county environmental health department. The roof of the motel was in very bad shape as well.

The first contact with the new owners was to have them apply for a license but I informed them to bring the motel up to regulations before I could issue a license and therefore they could not rent out any rooms. They were not happy to hear this and they went to work to try and bring the place into compliance. Eventually, they did get the smoke detectors working, fire equipment in place, and proper linens for the rooms. Some of the air conditioners were still not working and I issued the license with the stipulation that rooms without working air conditioners could not be rented out unless at a reduced rate.

The last time I saw these owners on the property, the frail gentleman was trying to put a cover over an opening for the air conditioner on a room and I told him that what he was doing looked like a temporary fix. He explained to me that he was doing the best he could but the place was up for sale and he thought he had a buyer.

The next time I came to the property there were two men on the roof with some other people and they were reproofing the building. One yelled down to some women on the parking lot saying with a broken accent, "Hey, here's that skinny inspector!"

As I got out of my car, a smiling lady came toward me with her hand extended and greeted me with a pleasant accent and said, "Hello, I'm Maria and we just bought the place."

I introduced myself and started to bring out the packet for change of license. She was quick to introduce her husband, Krystopher, and her brother in-law Stanley on the roof. There were three boys running around bringing materials and things to the men on the roof but I didn't pay much attention to them at the time. They went back to work and Maria and I went to the motel office to discuss the license process.

We discussed the past owners and how much I was looking forward to seeing the property being improved. She was assuring me that they had seen the past inspection reports and they wanted to see the property improve themselves. This was going to be there home and they were going to see the work completed by them and done properly.

She then told me they were all from Poland. They had lived in New Jersey for a while and bought the property as a long-term investment between brothers and family. I was very impressed with their attitude and was looking forward to see the changes they were promising to make. I let them know that I would help them in any way I could and left them with materials on the regulations and requirements for motel operators. The meeting was quick and I told them that I would be back for a change of ownership inspection as soon as I got a call from them when they were ready.

One month passed and I received a call from the Poprawski's that their motel the Palms Motel in Hope Sound was ready for the change of ownership and opening inspection. I drove to the location and almost drove past the location because I could not believe the change in the property. Everything had a new coat of paint. Exterior walls, doors, and the new roof changed the appearance of the place. A sign had been erected in front of the motel with a vacancy sign illuminating the bottom and rates posted as well.

I was greatly surprised and completed the change of ownership without any major problems. The pool had been addressed with a fresh coat of paint as well and papers were shown to me assuring that a licensed contractor was attending to the septic plant on a regular basis. All seemed in order and the Poprawski's were now the proud owners of the Palms Motel.

The motel was to be one of the finest improving establishments on my inventory of motel properties. Each time I would inspect the property I would find another improvement and there was always something going on with new mattress, new beds, furniture, drapes, or pool furnishings being added. One day the driveway was being resurfaced and the markings for parking spots were completed. Parking bumper blocks were painted in front of each motel room. The improvements seem to never stop.

It was late in 1989 I stopped to do an inspection and I started talking to the owners about a Polish girl I had just met. Krystopher, Maria's husband interrupted our conversation and excited said, "Oh, your going to marry that girl."

Maria and I usually did all the talking because her English was much better. I looked over at him and said, "I don't think so, and I just met her."

He replied, "You mark my words, you're going to marry this girl. What's her name?"

"Krystyna, she says she is from Warsaw, Poland," I replied.

"O.K., she going to make you a good wife and put some weight on that skinny body of yours, mark my words, I know about these Polish girls" Krystopher grinned a big toothy grin and laughed his way out the door.

Low and behold, Krystopher knew exactly what he was talking about. March 17, 1990 I married Krystyna. Maria and Krystopher was our Maid of Honor and Best Man which made me a little more nervous, but then I had been transferred out of the area and was no longer their inspector. We have maintained a relationship through the years even though the Poprawski's have moved on to other properties in the Ft. Lauderdale area. They have always improved every property they have owned and I am very proud of them.

The story goes as I can remember the Poprawski's invited Krystyna and I over for a dinner before the wedding day arrived. It was a typical Polish meal with all the trimmings including some beverage. It seems like whenever I left the table to get something or had to go to the restroom, I would come back to a full shot glass of vodka. I wanted to be sociable and didn't want to hurt anyone's feelings so I would empty the glass quickly and continue my meal. When it was time to say goodnight and complete all the thank you and good by, I felt my self-starting to sway back and forth.

When I went to the parking lot to find my car I dropped the car keys and started to pick them up. That is when I looked up and said to Krystyna, "We are not leaving here tonight. I am to drunk."

There was a room right in front of us and I turned to Poprawski's and said may I rent room 999? They said sure, just return the key in the morning. The Palms Motel had a complete number of 27 rooms. I was not so drunk that I was seeing double, but I was drunk enough to be seeing triple. We often joke about room 999 and I never make them feel so sociable again.

CHAPTER 14

VOLUNTEERING

It came about that one of our inspectors on the west coast had some serious health problem and they wanted an inspector from the east coast to travel over to the Ft. Myers area and stay for a month or so. They were not sure for how long the area would be in need of another inspector but hoped to find one of us that would be free enough to go. From my military experience I was always warned not to volunteer. This case was to be an exception and I really enjoyed working in the new area of Ft. Myers.

I let my boss know that I might be able to stay in a house my uncle had left to the Mormon Church if it was still there on the Peace River. I contacted relatives up north and they told me to go ahead but I would have to cut my way in, as the property had been vacant for so long. I would find a simplex mower in the shed and I could cut the grass to pay for the accommodations. This made the trip even more intriguing as I had never seen the house.

Off I went with all the street cards for the area and the print out of the establishments expecting everything to go so smoothly. When I got to the property to check in all the neighbors greeted me. They wanted to know if I had inherited the land and if they could buy their boat slips from me. I told them that I was a distant nephew and didn't know anything about boat slips. I was just here to stay for a few months and tend to the property, which really needed attention. The grass in the yard was waist deep and was surrounded by huge tall royal palm trees.

I checked in setting my suitcase in one room and making a bed with my sheets and blanket I had brought along. I looked throughout the home and found it to be large and interesting. My uncle had built the home I was raised in and I could tell this home had many of his trademarks. There was a servant's quarter, as my uncle lived a very long life, and an area between the servant's quarters and the main house left unexplored at this time.

The next morning I set out very early to travel the ten miles to Ft. Myers area. It was very busy in that it was the tourist season and traffic was extremely heavy. I found my first restaurant and completed an inspection prior to nine o'clock in the morning. By ten o'clock I found a fast food place and completed another. Things seemed to be moving along O.K. until I wanted to go across the bridge to Ft. Myers Beach. Traffic was deadlocked, bumper-to-bumper, crawling inch at a time until twelve o'clock noon. There I found a lodging to inspect.

Talking with the owners of the lodging place they told me to leave my car in their lot and travel on foot for the rest of the day. Great advice and I was able to finish four more lodging places before I called it a day. The last challenge was crossing over the bridge again on my way home. Boy, I wished I had brought a bike or a scooter for this route.

Back home I finished my paperwork and decided I had better give that tractor a try out in the shed. The grass was so high, I found the tractor would only cut in first gear and I knew it would have to be cut again and again to look like it should be. I also had to rake a lot of the grass in piles. Not even a third was cut and I had to call it a day.

But, the area was later to be such a joy to work because everyone was in such a festive mood and it felt like everyone was enjoying a vacation as well as me. The Sanibel Island was so beautiful with quaint lodging of bed and breakfast, rooming houses, and very small motels. It seemed like they would never end but the staff and owners were so friendly, we enjoyed the work all together. I was being complimented all the time for having answers to questions they needed for so many months and years,

On the Captiva Island I met the general manager of the resort there who shared the same last name. I did not let it influence me and he appreciated all the necessary violations I found in his food service establishment as well as the lodging. The only difficulty; I knew I would have to return through the obstacle course of tourist traffic. Homeward bound by four in the afternoon again.

Home and back at the lawn cutting and I had completed half of the job. One of the scariest incidences was when a huge black indigo snake crossed my path. I think he was angry that I was cutting his hiding place down. I had nightmares that evening. I would put the rest off till the weekend so I knew I would complete the lawn.

The restaurants were not in to bad a shape, as they knew what was expected and were geared up for a busy tourist season. Everyone was happy, owners making money, waitresses and staff busy making money, and the tourists were getting what they were paying for. The lodging people were always so grateful to see me and restaurant people welcomed me as if I had always been working in the area. I never came across a situation where I could not get someone attention or was questioned or interrupted from discussing new regulations or procedures recommended by the department.

Many of the owners were worried about their old inspector as to his health and if he was going to return. I could not advise them very well because all I had heard was of his status through the main office in Ft. Lauderdale. I proceeded to reach as many places in a day to stay on schedule and look forward to a weekend of work around the property on the Peace River.

TGIF and I headed home to the Peace River even not stopping or thinking about how bad the traffic was. I was so tired that I decided to let the yard work go until

Saturday morning. Instead, I headed up to the little one room restaurant on the edge of the Peace River next to the boat ramp. Entering the establishment I decided not to let them know what I did for a living and just pretend I was a tourist. But, the word had spread and they knew I was staying at my uncle's house. They all knew my uncle as he had built almost every building in the sub-division.

They were all full of questions and it seems those boat slips were built by my cousins and my uncle and were being rented to all the occupants. Little did I realize they thought I was the rich heir to all this. I tried to keep quiet and didn't say too much. I was observing the many violations in the place but not my business as it was in another district and out of my area. The most obvious was the lack of proper hood and ventilation. It didn't make the hamburgers taste any different and the fries were just the same as usual. Still the haze over the pool table mixed with the cigarette and cigar smoke didn't help my pool game either.

Saturday morning I did some more exploring in that area between the house and the servant's quarters to find a laundry room in back with washer and dryer. Down the hallway I leaned on a wall and it moved! I pushed and it rotated to open and as I peered in there was this carpeted room with an air conditioner. The carpet appeared to have rings from barrels and empty pallets. Then it dawned on me that this was an Armageddon Room as my uncle was a devout Mormon.

Just between the Armageddon Room and the shed was this huge tank full of water. There was a pipe leading into the top and pipes leading out of the bottom and into the house. I later found out this was an aeration system to remove the sulfur from the water. My uncle was the most ingenious individual I have ever known and no wonder he retired as an experimental engineer from General Motors when he was sixty-five years old. He moved to Florida, built this sub-division, became a member of the Mormon Church, and died at ninety-nine. I really felt happy when I finished the lawn and someone came by the property and picked up the stacks of grass left between the royal palms.

Monday, I was back to work trying to cross the bridge onto Ft. Myers Beach and finding a parking spot. The rest of the day I enjoyed completing one whole side of the beach area that had lodgings. It looked like it was going to be a very good week ahead and I was thinking of traveling back to the east coast that coming Friday.

I checked in with the main office in Ft. Lauderdale and they told me to think about staying a bit longer as the inspector in that area had to undergo more tests and treatment. I said I needed to go back to my home for the weekend but would return on Sunday.

The drive back to the area from the east coast was longer than I remember and I didn't pull into my uncle's drive until dark. It was a bit eerie entering his home but I said, "Uncle George, it's just me." I was so tired I just fell off to sleep.

Monday, I set up my days work on Sanibel and drove directly to the first location. Again, I was greeted warmly and completed the work to stay on schedule. Much of the time was spent on answering questions and assuring them that they would have their regular inspector back very soon. I was wondering if it would ever rain over on the west coast or did they always have this sunny perfect for tourist weather. It did make it nice to work in this atmosphere and kept everyone in an uplifting spirit.

Back at the uncle's home, I explored the neighborhood and listened to the tales about my uncle. The neighbors all had heart-warming stories of how he helped them all to become owners or helped them financially or just gave them food when they needed it. I never heard so many good things about Uncle George but he was that uncle that sold my folks our home at a very low price and had candy in his overcoat pockets every time he came for the mortgage payment of seventeen dollars a month.

It happened that one of the neighbors had a sixteen-foot boat with an Evinrude outboard motor, and lots of toys on the dash (compass, horn, bilge pump, and depth finder). My son was enrolled in a marine mechanics class in school and my thought was it might be a good experience for him. One of the weekends I brought my son over to the Peace River, we picked up the boat and drove back to the east coast.

When I had completed the inventory of restaurants and lodging in the Ft. Myers area I returned to my own area quite concerned about falling behind. I found out that some supervisor had come up from Ft. Lauderdale and picked up some of the establishments. I cannot say it was not appreciated but I was worried if the inspections were good enough.

At the end of the fiscal year my supervisor called me into the office with the director. They wanted to show me some letters the district had received from the Ft. Myers area. There were two from restaurant owners and four from hotel and motel owners. Some were on the Ft. Myers Beach, three from Sanibel and one from Captiva. They were all telling the department how much they appreciated and liked the inspector that called on their establishment in the last quarter. They expressed their satisfaction on the way the inspections were conducted and mostly the way the inspector helped them with questions and problems they were having. I was shocked but at the same time very proud of the job I was able to do for the inspector that eventually had to quit due to his illness.

My director told me the letters would be entered into my file and sent to Tallahassee for the personnel files. I was given copies to take home with me as well. What I felt was a situation that I volunteered for turned into a much-needed enjoyable vacation and a plus for my career as a health inspector.

CHAPTER 15

FOOD BORNE ILLNESS

Health Inspectors have an extensive series of training in all faces of their job. The training is continuous and scheduled usually on a monthly basis. Over the many years the program has taken on new and then has changed to reduce the amount of responsibilities. But in the beginning the health inspector was trained in environmental public health issues, food service issues, public lodging issues, and fire safety protection including certification training and testing.

Because the health inspector was to be knowledgeable in all of these areas the training had to be conducted on a monthly basis usually at district offices or scheduled at seminars combining more than one district. Each training class would be followed by a test and scores announced before you left the training. If you failed to pass there would be a retraining for those that needed it and a retest before you were allowed to continue work.

The most extensive training program is when the health inspectors were given the certification as special fire inspectors. This was held in Ocala with Fire

Marshal instructors that followed a special booklet that covered everything from construction to hood systems for food service establishments. The program covered the knowledge of entrance in and out of buildings of all sorts of occupancy. It covered the sprinkler systems, suppression systems, and building materials acceptable for safe construction. The instructional course lasted an entire week and testing was extensive and completed before you left the training.

Upon passing this special fire training you were issued a certification that was to be carried with the health inspector at all times and to be renewed each year until retesting at a five year interval. The classes were very helpful and any questions or problems that may arise during the inspectors caring out their inspection could be quickly resolved by a call to the fire marshal's office in Ocala. The certification also gave the health inspector a degree of respect from local fire departments as we tried to work together on problems that might come to light during the state restaurant or lodging inspection.

The health inspector had to be trained and very knowledgeable about food borne illnesses. This was a continual training program an inspector would be sent information from district office and training pamphlets issued during monthly district meetings. The pamphlets were used as resource tools and were always kept in files that the inspector could carry in their vehicles.

It was always great when an inspector could attend a seminar on food borne illness and have the opportunity to see the product or source immediately. One of the best seminars held in Orlando was conducted by the Florida Department of Fish and Game. They brought many samples of fish and shellfish products for the inspector to handle and identify. It is one thing to read about a disease caused by a particular food product but is another thing to see it first hand and stays with the inspector much longer.

Ciguatera is a food borne illness caused by eating certain reef fish whose flesh is contaminated with toxins originally produced by dinoflagellates such as Gambierdiscus toxicus, which lives in tropical and subtropical waters. This is basically a food borne illness caused by eating reef fish in waters that have been contaminated and has moved through the food chain after the fish have consumed the algae and seaweed from these reefs.

Symptoms of Ciguatera can be headaches, muscle aches, vomiting, vertigo, and hallucinations. There can also be possible neurological symptoms where hot foods taste cold and cold foods taste hot. 1

A food borne illness case I had to investigate was made much easier with the knowledge gained from this particular seminar. The case informed a couple who had experienced all the symptoms of ciguatera. The restaurant advertised as their special, Black Grouper. The investigation found that the product came from a fishery in Miami but originated from an unlicensed fisherman working the reefs on the east coast of the Caribbean islands. This is a no fishing allowed area because it is known to have contaminated reefs.

The unfortunate problem of getting ciguatera is there is no known cure other than over time the symptoms will wear off. It can be as long as two or three years. The restaurant owner was told to remove the product from sale, informed of the source of the product, and eventually had to settle in court with the complainants.

Salmonella is the most common form of food borne illness. Salmonellosis is an infection with Salmonella bacteria. Most people infected with Salmonella develop diarrhea, fever, vomiting, and abdominal cramps 12 to 72 hours after infection. Most cases the infected person will recover with four to seven days without treatment. Sometimes diarrhea can be so severe patient become dangerously dehydrated and must be hospitalized.

Sources of salmonella can be poultry, pork, and beef, if the meat is prepared incorrectly or is infected with the bacteria after preparation. Infected eggs, egg products, and milk when not prepared, handled, or refrigerated properly. Reptiles, such as turtles, lizards, and snakes, which may carry the bacteria in their intestines, are sources of the salmonella. Also tainted fruits and vegetables can have the salmonella bacteria. 2

1 – Ciguatera, from Wikipedia, the fee encyclopedia.
2 – Salmonellosis, from Wikipedia, the free encyclopedia.

The most complex case of salmonella outbreak as an inspector in my district occurred at a bar restaurant operated by an owner that would not cooperate with the regulators and eventually had to go out of business. The salmonella infection started with poultry product left unprotected from proper refrigeration outside the backdoor of his establishment. The product was brought into the establishment, handled by several food prep personnel, spread to other staff members, which spread the salmonella through out the surfaces in the establishment. Eventually the customers came in contact with the bacteria and finally even the owner.

The blame did not only belong to the owner but to the regulators that left the establishment without an inspector for a long period of time. This was due to the slow down in hiring and therefore the restaurant did not receive the attention and regulation it should have had. The owner would not listen to the regulators once the outbreak was discovered and tried to stay open without completing a thorough sanitization of the property. This cost him his business and the salmonella incident was a case study of what not to do.

Shigella is a genus of Gram-negative, nonspore forming, non-motile, rod-shaped bacteria closely related to Salmonella. The causative agent of human shigellosis, Shigella causes disease in primates, but not in other mammals. It is only naturally found in human and apes. During infection, it typically causes dysentery. The genus is named after Kiyoshi Shiga, who first discovered it in 1898. 3

As an inspector I first was aware of the threat of Shigella while early in my career as a health inspector we had the responsibility of inspecting childcare facilities.

Shigella bacteria is most commonly found with baby's feces and contracted by caregivers without sanitary practices of wearing gloves while changing diapers or washing hands thoroughly and properly after the task is completed. Shigella bacteria can spread very fast from hand to hand when hand washing facilities are not provided and hand washing procedures are not practiced with proper sanitation.

This was also apparent to me as a health inspector when a very popular and prominent restaurant was reported to our district as having six patrons diagnosed as having the Shigella bacteria. My previous inspections had noted a lack of paper towels and proper hand washing soap at all of the hand washing sinks. My hindsight told me I was to lacks with the operator and should have brought them for hearing at the least, after the second notice of the same violation.

Because I was the health inspector the investigation was conducted by a local nurse from the county health department and assisted by me. Each employee and patron affected was interviewed and statements charted showing what was prepared or consumed. The final story was two patrons and their babies ate salad at the restaurant. They went home and their husbands both contracted the Shigella bacteria. The food prep

3 – Shigella, from Widipedia, the free encyclopedia

employee that made the salad had just left home after taking care of her baby and the neighbor's baby (both babies had shigella bacteria) and reported to work. She did not wash her hands because there were no soap or paper towels for her and she was running late anyway. The owner settled out of court for a sum around six thousand dollars.

Escherichia coli Gram-negative bacteria found I feces; frequently causing inflammation of the bowel, peritonitis, or cystitis. Also called E-coli. 4

These bacteria can be very deadly as witnessed in the outbreak in Seattle. As health inspectors we were all trained to understand the E-coli bacteria incident and watched many films on the cause and effect. It was our responsibility to educate the food service industry about the results of undercooked meats and improper handling of products that can come in contact with E-coli. Bulletins were issued on a regular basis from Federal agencies whenever there were outbreaks or products found with the E-coli bacteria present. The bulletins would be handed out by the health inspectors or mailed to the food service establishments as soon as they were issued.

Hepatitis A – Liver inflammation caused by a virus. It can be contracted through contaminated food, by receiving a transfusion of infected blood, or other causes. A vaccine against the disease is available. 5

I was the health inspector that had the establishment who hired a Jamaican busboy with the Hepatitis A virus. At the first sign of illness he was sent to the hospital and tested for the virus. He then was removed from employment and all other employees at the restaurant were tested. No other cases appeared but the restaurant took immediate offensive actions to combat the negative results of the media attention. The restaurant installed several talking hand sinks that kept track of each employee and recorded their hand washing activities. The sink spoke the language of the employee and printed a document at the end of the day to verify the employee by name and the number of times they would use the hand sink. The sinks even alarmed the employee if they past the sink without washing their hands when needed. The restaurant was a national chain establishment with a reputation that is highly regarded and is still doing very well today.

The hepatitis virus is well known in my background not only as a health inspector but my sister in-law came to the United States from Poland and did not know how she contracted hepatitis. The strain was referred to as non-A and non-B but did extensive damage to her liver. She was given 24 hours to receive a liver transplant or she would die. Fortunately the University of Nebraska Medical Center in Omaha, Nebraska received her in time and she got a liver transplant. During the operation her kidneys did not return to a functional state and a year later she had a kidney transplant. Fifteen years later the kidney failed and I was able to donate one of my kidneys. This is why a portion of the funds from this book will go to the Transplant Patient Assistance Program at UNMC in Omaha, Nebraska.

4 – Escherichia coli, The New American Medical Dictionary and Health Manual.

5 – Hepatitis A, The New American Medical Dictionary and Health Manual.

There was another outbreak from an illness that could not be defined while I was a health inspector. The restaurant was a building that I had worked in many years before becoming a health inspector. At that time in my life I was a Howard Johnson Manager. The building was bought by a new operator and made into a seafood restaurant with very special gourmet dishes. The restaurant was open for less than six months and a phone call came to the owner saying the person ate at the restaurant and they were in the hospital with some kind of illness. The owner took the person at their word but the news spread and several others started to call in to the restaurant with the same complaint. The owner had never dealt with this type of situation before and he made a very bad mistake. Instead of calling the health inspection department he called the media. By the next day over two hundred cases were reported, more than he served, and some were asking where the restaurant was located.

The investigation found that a disgruntled employee that was fired threw some kind of chemical into the ice machine. The restaurant could not survive the class action suet and had to close their doors months later.

CHAPTER 16

ROAD TO INDIANTOWN

It is a sultry hot day as I head west on Highway 76 out of Stuart. The road changes names from Colorado Avenue in Stuart, to Kanner Highway from Stuart to I-95, and then is known as Highway 76 till it goes past Indiantown to Lake Okeechobee.

The first stop will be a Ripper's Deli at the corner of 701 that leads to Pratt Whitney to the south. Here at Rippers I will meet a sweet bunch of girls that are busy setting up for a day of serving lunches to all the workers out west of town. Rippers are known for homemade freshly squeezed lemonade. They will add a little sweetener to the large container and it will last all the way to Indiantown.

Back on Highway 76 you must travel the speed limit but look out for those truck of workers with their dual wheels in the back because they will be pushing you to speed up or they will be passing you on this two lane road. Highway 76 parallels the Saint Lucie Canal that connects the St. Lucie River with Lake Okeechobee. As you travel the road looking to the north you may see a large sailing vessel or a large yacht that will have to pass through at least two sets of locks. The locks were built by the Army Corp of Engineers to facilitate the difference in water levels between the lakes and Saint Lucie River.

About halfway to Indiantown there is a stop to make at a horse boarding and training area where there is a kitchen to serve the groomers, riders, and the owners of the horses. The place is a little rustic but the operators are trying there best to make food available to a clientele that are pretty much stranded out there. Hot sandwiches, chili, soup, and sodas are provided. Sometimes they have a special of rice and beans or macaroni and cheese. The staff is very conscious of the requirements of training, temperature controls, and storage procedures. Inspections are always complied with a few minor violations.

Back out to Highway 76 you have to show the guard at the entrance of the horse facility again to leave. Once he raises the barrier you will look both ways and proceed with caution because the entrance is on a long curve in the road.

The ride is pleasant and if the occasional vessel passes on the canal you will slow down a bit to enjoy the view. The boat passengers will always wave and you will give them a quick wave back but keeping your eye on the road for the wild animal that might scurry across in front of you. There is a large mobile home park on the left and this is where a lot of people live that work the farms, fruit groves, and labor jobs around Indiantown.

One can see the overpass of Indiantown Road as it crosses Highway 76 and you see the flashing caution light at the left hand turn to reach the overpass. Just to the right is small cut with a little bridge on the highway. Here is where I saw a dead alligator that tried to cross the road but must have been hit by a truck or something. A quick thought was to throw it in the back of my trunk and then I knew that is against the law.

So onward to the left turn at the caution light and make the turn to the stop sign at Indiantown Road. Then you cross the overpass and the name of the road is Warfield Blvd. You will see to the left the revolving railroad bridge that opens to let the boat travel pass and closes when the train rolls alongside Indiantown Road.

The first stop was a restaurant that is probably not open anymore. The best thing I guess I could say about this stop was that sometimes there would be saddles laying on the sidewalk by the front door and once inside I looked around the dining room and noticed I was the only one not wearing cowboy boots. An ex-truck driver and his wife were running the restaurant but they really didn't have the heart for restaurant business. I always had trouble with the temperatures in their refrigeration units that were all on their last leg.

Then on to the next restaurant, where I could hardly wait to tell them about the gator on Highway 76, because they had a road kill menu hanging on the wall. They all sounded interested in the gator but I didn't see anyone racing out the back door or jumping into their pickup to leave. This was a nice clean place where you could get a good home cooked meal for a very reasonable price. The building belonged to the WW Lumber Company in Indiantown and there had been many different restaurants as the operators tried to make a go of it but never seemed to stay.

Next on the list was the Seminole Inn. Mr. Warfield, who owned the railroad that passed through Indiantown, built the Inn. This historic structure was built for the Duke of Windsor who advocated the English throne and his bride, Miss Warfield-Simpson. They were to stay at the Inn on their honeymoon. Unfortunately the couple never stayed in the Inn but did visit it once.

The Inn had fallen in disrepair over the years and had been badly operated until the Wall family of WW Lumber took over the ownership. I remember the opening inspection, as Mr. Wall was not feeling well and remained in the Windsor dining room while his beautiful young daughter took me on the tour. They had decorated each room with a different motif and furnished each room with antique furniture. It was a wonderful collection of antiques that must have set Mr. Wall back a few dollars.

Mr. Wall was quite upset with the dress his daughter chose to wear for this occasion. You see he was also a minister and his daughter who had traveled the world wore a very shear full-length antique dress with a wide brim hat. She looked like the lady of the Inn and was sweat as can be for a southern girl.

Trying not to be distracted I checked out all the smoke detectors in each room, the fire extinguishers, and the pull stations located throughout the hallways. As we entered each room she would run over to the window to pull back the curtain or window dressing to let the sun shine in. It would also distract my attention on that beautiful shear dress she wore. All in all the Inn was in great shape like its matron and I was about to give it a final O.K. Then I said open this door at the end of the hallway where there was an exit sign brightly lit. There was the fire escape that was pulled up from the ground floor. It was very rusty and I could tell it needed repair. There was another on the other wing that was in the same shape.

I went downstairs to talk to Mr. Wall and first complemented him on the fine job of having the Inn almost complete for final inspection and licensing. He was upset but totally understood about the fire escapes and promised to have them rebuilt and ready within two days. He was a minister at his word and a fine southern gentleman. The license was issued the following two day.

I love to inspect the Inn as it has so much history with it and there seems always to be something new or different each time I go there. The beautiful floor in the Windsor dining room used to have a problem on one end as the floor would warp and rise up. It was finally repaired. The wallpaper in the men's bathroom would always give me the opportunity to tell Mr. Wall's daughter that there were flies in the bathroom. She knew exactly what I meant as the design on the wallpaper was fishing flies for the fly fisherman.

The dining room with a bar appeared in a movie made by Burt Reynolds several years ago and revamped back to its original dining. Several glass doors along the one wall open to a backyard surrounded by a garden walk. The Sunday buffet is served in this room. There is a swimming pool outside but it constantly gave the owners problems because it was to old and when they tried to improve it there was problems with the permits and paperwork.

I hope you will take a trip to Indiantown to enjoy this nice Inn, its staff, and a good meal.

CHAPTER 17

BOOKER PARK

There is an area on the other side of the tracks from The Seminal Inn. This area is past the Indiantown Martin County Sheriff's office and just a left hand turn from Indiantown Road. One would cross the railroad tracks and continue down the street to find Booker Park. This area was one of the highest crime areas in Indiantown and was populated by the labor force for the farmland, citrus grove, and sugar cane industries.

These residents usually worked for minimum wage or below and spent most of their money on rent, food, and lottery tickets. They were the poorest of the poor and lived in very sub standard conditions to say the least. The housing was usually a large rooming house or a two by four constructed eight by eight foot building with a tin roof. A prominent lawyer practicing law on the coast owned the rooming house. He was born in raised in Booker Park and he always wanted to give back to the community because of his roots. A couple that continuously worked on the units and collected rent from an office-convenient store located on the same property owned the tin roof buildings.

First the rooming house was rented to migrants and low-income people and they spent most of their weekends drinking, partying, and destroying the property. If there was a fire it was used to keep warm or roast some food. This gave the residence the excuse to use the fire extinguishers located on the outside of the building or they were removed for selling at the local pawnshops. I had a meeting with the owner in his law office and explained as long as he maintained the building; replacing the missing or discharged fire extinguishers, broken glass windows, or removing broken bottles and trash from around the building, he would not have any problems with me.

Now, the county wanted the building torn down. They never gave it a thought as to where these people would find shelter. They just wanted the nuisance removed. Eventually, the lawyer collected his damages and sold the building. The building was finally demolished and the land left barren.

The tin roof buildings numbered in the thirties and would continually go down in number as some burned, the people themselves destroyed some and some by Mother Nature. The owner would try to rebuild one and another would disappear. It always amazed me that the building could pass any building code, as they did not even have inner walls. The electrical was just very basic with maybe a light bulb and an electrical switch

My experience in this neighborhood was varied and it grew increasingly hard to accept giving the owner additional time to correct violations. He was amiable and tried to correct every violation by the required time. It seemed as if it were a loosing battle in that there were always additional damage to be corrected on every return visit.

One visit I had to make was on a complaint given to us by the local health department. They were treating a resident that lived in a tin roof unit. She was in a wheel chair for spinal injuries and was assisted in and out of bed by an assistant that would come to her each day. It seems she had rat bites on her feet and was receiving treatment for them at the health department.

When I went to see her they told me I would find her in the local bar and pool hall. Sure enough there she was inside the establishment. I asked her to please come outside to talk to me and show me where she lived. We proceed to the tin roof unit and she showed me inside. I didn't really go inside but observed the light coming through the holes on the bottom of the back wall and through knotholes large enough for rats to enter.

This should have been enough for any inspector but I had to go around behind the unit to see for myself the paths that were left by these rats.

Bad move on my part. The holes were obvious with lots of gnawing marks and dropping left by the rats. The weeds I had to wade through to get there left me with jiggers. This was to cause me great pain for over six months. I will never forget the incident. The owner was summoned so

I could show him the torture this girl was going through and he was instructed to clean up the grounds around the unit as well as sealing all the rat holes.

There were additional apartment buildings where there were a row of units that had bigger rooms and sometimes two or three rooms to one unit. These buildings were all wood structures on concrete slabs. The owner owned a small market in Booker Park and would make repairs as I turned in the inspection reports to her. The thing that always stood out was the number of satellite dishes on the roof of these units. I could never understand how they could afford such luxury but with all the number of people that would live in one unit, I guess anything was possible.

My greatest joy was working in Booker Park around the holidays. I would always make a point of filling my pockets with candy and the barefooted kids would come running after me as I tried to see everyone would get some sweat candy.

One day I locked my keys inside my vehicle and had to call one of my fellow inspectors who lived close by me. I asked him to please go to my home and bring me a spare set to unlock the car. He finally came in the afternoon, but I had walked the entire Booker Park area that day to complete my inspections. When he arrived he said he had only read about Booker Park and had never been there. He was scared as could be and left right away. I was never scared, even though I had heard about the crime, and I always treated each of them, as I would want to be treated. That is all they asked of me.

CHAPTER 18

SAVING MY LIFE

It only occurred once in the twenty-four years working as a health inspector but it was not an incident I will likely forget. I was informed of an illegal rooming house operating in Booker Park. The county inspector was working on a case where there was a child being treated for hepatitis and she was supposed to be residing in this unlicensed facility. The inspector asked me to accompany her to the property as she looked in on the child and I could observe the situation myself.

I was not sure at first because the inspector did not hesitate to enter the building without knocking or saying anything to introduce herself. She turned to me and said to come on in because there was no one around. We entered a rundown building with broken boards on the porch and posts missing from a railing that surrounded the porch. Inside the hallway was quite dark with only the light from the back door giving a glow into the room in the back. We passed several doors on each side of the hallway until we came to a room that looked like a dining area and kitchen.

Under the table was a little dirty blonde haired girl. She was crouched down on one knee and on her little bare foot was crawling a palmetto bug. The lady inspector reached down and swiped it off the little girls foot and asked her to come out and speak to us. She was quite shy but did come out brushing her tangled hair back off her face. I just wanted to pick her up and take her to a bath and wash her hair. She looked ill and the lady inspector asked her how she was feeling.

She was alone, and she looked like she might be six or seven years old. How could this child be here in this horrible place without an adult around? Suddenly a girl came through the open door from the back yard. She grabbed the little girl and said she was her mother. The girl inspector explained that she had stopped to see how the little girl was doing as she was asked to by the nurses at the clinic. She also explained why I was there.

I had seen enough and knew that my immediate response was to go to my car and post a citation on the property. The notice would say that this building was operated as an unlicensed rooming house and must be brought into compliance as soon as possible. It was just about the time I got to my car when a big car pulled into the front yard slamming on its brakes and sending stones and grass from its path.

Out jumped this woman dressed in a wrinkled housedress as she jumped up on the porch from the opening at the end. Then she raised her hand towards the two of us holding a very large pistol. She screamed at the two of us to get off her property. We had no right to enter her building and we must leave. I stopped and told her there was no need for a gun in this matter. All I needed to do was post a sign on the door of the building. She said that she was the owner and no sign was necessary. We were to leave or I will shoot you where you are standing. You are on my property and I have the right to protect it.

I told her I was getting into my car and I will be back with a Sheriff Deputy. It didn't take me more than ten minutes and the patrol car pulled up next to her car with the flashers going and I parked where I had been before in front of the building.

The deputy called her by her name and said to lower her gun right now. She did not listen to him as she again threatened to shoot me. I told the deputy that I didn't get paid enough to put up with this and all I need to do is post a sign on the building. He explained to the owner that I would be posting the sign on the porch post and would be leaving immediately. I could tell she was not happy and she let me post the sign and then said for me to get now.

The three of us went back to the Sheriff's office on Indiantown Road and each of us filled out reports on the incident. The deputy filled one out also. All these reports will be put into a report file for the day and someday there would be action by the court. The charges listed on the report were assault on a police officer and threatening a public official.

A year later I received a subpoena to appear in court on a certain date. The day came and I received another call telling me I did not have to appear because the case was dismissed due to lack of evidence. It seems the files in the Sheriff's office were missing so the judge had no other choice but to dismiss the case.

The only other time I came close to violence happened behind a police station when I was about to inspect a small restaurant. I noticed some fellows unloading bundles from the truck of a car and didn't pay much attention to them. The next thing I knew, about ten police cars were surrounding both our cars with their lights flashing and sirens blaring.

I did my best to let them know that I was caught in the middle of this and I was there to inspect the restaurant in front of us. They let me leave the area and I went back later in the day to find a relieved restaurant owner. Business was not to good for him that day.

CHAPTER 19

BEYOND INDIANTOWN

Just before turning to the left and crossing the railroad tracks to enter Booker Park, there was a right hand turn off from Warfield Blvd. There on the immediate left side of the road was a group of tin roofed migrant housing buildings that were always full. The driveway was ruff dirt and dust. I felt bad when I pulled in with my state vehicle because it always raised a lot of dust and the kids would scatter from the driveway and some of the adults would scatter to the inside of the buildings or around back out of sight. I knew they might have thought I was an INS official.

The inside of the buildings were very roughly constructed with inside toilet facilities, kitchen sink, stove, refrigerator, wooden floors and walls that were left unfinished. There was a time when I had to go inside one of the units and I found sleeping bags lined up on the floor, garbage bags overflowing in the kitchen, and questionable electrical wiring that I wrote on the report for the landlord to be aware of the violation.

Re-inspections always found the violations corrected but the dust was always there. The landlord had provided coin operated washer and dryer for the residents but I was always finding the ladies washing their clothes from a bucket and rubbing them against the lid to a septic tank behind the buildings. They can leave their home country but you can't take their home country habits from them.

This was one of the places I was always greeted at Christmas time because the children knew my pockets were full of candy. It made me feel very good and full of the Christmas spirit as those barefooted little kids came running up to the car and followed me until my pockets were empty. They all had the whitest teeth with the biggest smiles and their innocence told the story of their riches.

There was a time I was requested by the State to investigate a wild game resort in the Northwest corner of Martin County. It was reported they were selling wild venison meat to restaurants. I was aware of Harry and the Natives having venison on his menu and knew he was getting the product from the preserve. So I drove to the location and was greeted at the gate by a wild water buffalo. Not a statue but a real buffalo. Later, a zebra ran by the car, an ostrich, and then I saw a large herd of African deer roll over the plains and disappear behind the vegetation. Before I got to the main lodge, I passed an airport landing strip and thought how cool is this.

I pulled up to what looked like the main lodge and was greeted by a young lady that confirmed that I had arrived at my destination. She said her husband would be right out to show me around after I had shown her my identification. The gentleman came to see me and offered to show me around. They had the main lodge, four guest quarters in separate buildings, and a meat processing plant. I had only to look at the processing plant and ask a few questions. First did they have a licensed veterinarian? Yes, his son was the vet to inspect the wild animal meat immediately after the kill. Second was the processing plant inspected by the Department of Agriculture? Yes, they have been inspected and licensed by that department.

I watched as they cryovacted some fresh venison and turned down an offer to accept a steak or two. After his explanation of their entire operation, I was satisfied that I had seen enough. He explained to me how much he appreciated having the opportunity to show his place to me and he also appreciated what a beautiful day it was outside. It seems he just got out of the federal penitentiary because someone landed on his airstrip with a load of drugs and he was sent away for a little vacation.

The county health department called me one day to ask if I would visit a home outside of Indiantown with one of their inspectors. It was a case of a child that was being treated by the county health department for hookworm. This was a new disease I was not familiar with and as we traveled out to the patient's home it was explained to me. We were greeted by a pack of kids and a pack of dogs surrounded by a bunch of farm animals when we arrived at what I could best describe as a wild ranch in the middle of nowhere.

We spoke to the mother of the pack of kids as she held her latest one in her arms. She seemed bothered by the fact that we were there but tried to understand what we were explaining to her. The child had to stop sleeping with the puppies, as the disease he had contracted could get progressively worse to a point where the child would go blind. She looked at us like we were crazy and stated all her children have slept with the puppies throughout their lives.

We left with the uneasy feeling that the problem would not be addressed and it might have to end up in the hands of another agency.

There was a time when I found furry claws sticking up at me as I lifted the lid on a freezer. I asked, "What is that?"

"Oh, that's our possum. That's our dinner special tonight!"

"Where did it come from?" I asked.

"We ran over it on the way in today. We all love to eat possum out here!"

"I'm sorry, not tonight", I responded.

It is a very different culture out west of the towns along the coast in Florida and one has got to respect them and they will return that respect. It was always a challenge and yet a fulfilling adventure that left many memories.

CHAPTER 20

RATS

The incredibly ugly times came when we had to investigate infestations of rodents or insects. The complaints would either come to the attention of the State Hotels and Restaurants inspections or in some cases a county complaint. The usual situation would be found during a normal inspection and roaches would be found inside the food prep area due to unclean sanitation practices or brought in from suppliers and never addressed immediately.

One of the worst infestations of roaches was at an oriental facility in a food court at the mall. The insects had spread to the back hallway and were entering other food establishments on both sides of the oriental place. The operator of the oriental restaurant did not want to accept his responsibility until we had him close down until a final inspection was satisfactory with no sign of an insect. Then he was to store all of his food off the floor as required by regulations and the establishment serviced by a licensed pest control contractor. The other food establishments in the same food court finally got their problem resolved also.

Usually an older establishment that has started to deteriorate over many years becomes a problem when it is located on the ocean shore. This was the case involving a beachfront resort located on Singer Island. The old resort was struggling to maintain itself as the newer resorts sprang up around the shoreline. The resort even extended its life by renting out a bar on the beach as a movie location starring a local celebrity.

It was after the movie was produced, I had to inspect the entire facility, the hotel and the bar on the beach. As usual the hotel manager, the housekeeping manager, and the food and beverage manager accompanied me throughout the inspection. We had competed the hotel sweep and filled the page with violations mostly covering deteriorated walls, fixtures, and bad linen. Now, we proceeded to the outside bar where they had a bikini clad little bar maid who was returning to the bar from delivering a drink to a couple on the beach. She quickly stooped under the bar as it did not have a lifted section on the bar and the only egress was to go under the bar, I supposed.

I followed her and the rest of my entourage waited outside the bar area. I was still around 135 pounds and could maneuver egress without any difficulty. My first comment was they should cut the bar and make a lift shelf to go in and out from behind the bar. I then went to move the wastebasket to see if they were keeping the bar floor area clean. I stopped suddenly and said, "That's not real?"

The manager's comment was, "What's not real?"

"That", I pointed to the biggest beach rat I had ever seen. He was the size of a small cat.

The little bartender in her little bikini took a quick glance down at the floor and she literally flew over the top of the bar. A new egress from behind the bar I had not envisioned.

We were to discover the rat was dead and had evidently consumed some of the rat poison the resort had placed around the area in boxes. The rat was removed by one of the maintenance personnel and the inspection completed with the usual violations of wine bottles stored in ice bins and the same ice used to serve in drinks, soda wands not cleaned properly, ice scoop buried in the ice so the bartender had to put her hands in the ice. My recommendation was to keep the doors to the bar seating area closed, which I knew they would never do until the bar was closed for the night.

The only good thing was the little bartender in the little bikini did not have to wear the flying nuns hat to egress from behind the bar. She did very well as she squealed all the way over the bar.

One of the ugly situations came from a complaint by the county health department concerning rodents in a restaurant the Department of Hotels and Restaurants had licensed and was responsible to inspect. The complaint was so serious the county wanted to send one of their supervisors to meet me at the restaurant. Fortunately, I knew the supervisor and we entered the establishment together.

We witnessed a long counter with a stove and refrigerator located directly behind the counter. There were four construction workers sitting at the counter eating soup. We also saw at the very end of the counter were about four mice sitting on the counter top and the last customer was throwing crackers down to them. Above the mice we could see ceiling tile missing and an open attic area above the mice.

We introduced ourselves showing our credentials and explained to the lady behind the counter why we were there. The men said they were the roofers working on the leaking room and we here for a lunch break. We told them not to stop and we would only be a minute to discus the problem. They didn't think there was a problem and continued to eat but their companions on the end of the counter scattered as we rounded the end.

The owner stated the mice had been coming in because the roof had large holes in it and was being invaded by the critters. I went over to her soup she had on the stove and lifted the ladle. To my surprise a big mother of all rats laid across the ladle. I was even more surprised as the customers kept right on eating their soup.

"Mam, do you realize this is in your soup?" I asked.

"Well, I just can't get rid of them!" She replied.

We had quite a time getting her to understand she had to close her restaurant until the situation was brought under control. She was insistent that we were being terribly unfair and that we were white and she was black and we were not treating her fairly. It took call to Tallahassee and she finally agreed to close voluntarily.

I still cannot believe the workers kept eating their soup and joined in the argument that we were discriminating against the poor owner. Unbelievable.

Sometimes, you wonder what it takes for an owner to understand the gravity of his business. There was a restaurant that had a very busy business of breakfast and lunch. I had inspected the facility for the first time and was concerned about a refrigeration unit at the front counter area that was not cold enough. There was fresh fish in the unit and I had him immediately remove the fish and put it in a working unit. He complied. Then I went to the back of the restaurant and found the back door open. I looked around the corners of the food prep area and witnessed rodent droppings throughout the area. The back door was closed and I set him up with a re-inspection to take place in seven days.

Seven days passed and I approached the restaurant from the rear door that I found propped wide open again. I first went to the front of the restaurant to meet the owner and he immediately said the refrigeration had been fixed. I checked the temperature and found it to be accurate. I then told him about his back door and he gave me the excuse that an order had just been received and they forgot to close it. We went to the food prep area and found a dead rat under their dish-machine, one in the storeroom, and one in a trap under the pass-through window. Three strikes and you are out. Hearing ordered and fine to be paid. Re-inspection after hearing found the rat problem solved but the refrigeration unit was again on the fritz.

CHAPTER 21

WORKING WITH THE INDUSTRY

In the beginning the goal of the Department of Hotels and Restaurants was protecting the public while working with the industry. I truly believed in the latter part of this program as I came from the industry with such a heavy background in management. I also had the experience of running many successful foodservice operations and my first position out of college was operating a 200-unit apartment complex. I was always aware of the assistance the managers and operators needed from the department.

The department had all kinds of handouts, brochures, and websites the inspectors were to make available to the operators or managers. This was fine but not conclusive because many-times the operators or managers still could not get their problems answered. They were so very grateful when they would get their problem resolved by the inspector himself.

It was so easy to just site the violation, give a warning, and leave the establishment for a return inspection. If on the return inspection the violation was uncorrected a hearing would be scheduled and fines imposed on an industry that could have used the money to correct the violation in time or improve his business after the violation was corrected.

It was common practice for the department to make special notice of the inspector that gave the most violations or brought the most hearings to the hearing officer. It was never recognized when an inspector helped an operator or manager solve his violation and therefore a hearing was not necessary. The only satisfaction was given to the inspector by the industry or his own personal satisfaction knowing he had helped the industry.

Such was the case in a small popular restaurant in my own hometown. The restaurant was continually in violation of improper storage of food in their very small walk-in refrigeration unit. The restaurant was in a shopping center on a corner location. The restaurant had a clientele of seniors from the local condo development as well as a thriving weekdays and Sunday after church business.

It happened that I discussed the situation with the owners and they had great fears of having to close the restaurant because of the cost of bringing in additional walk-in units that meant upwards in the thousands of dollars. I found a neighboring restaurant undergoing an extensive renovation and they had an exterior walk-in on a concrete slab available for sale.

I returned to the owner of the first restaurant with the negotiated terms and they could afford the new unit. I told them I could take the time on my weekend to show them the unit and assist with the transfer. When we arrived at the walk-in unit we were surprised to find a homeless man living inside. He was escorted from his temporary domicile and the moving process began.

The owner and manager were so pleased that their violations had been taken care of without having to go through the hearing and fine process. It made me feel like I had really lived up to my end of the bargain to work with the industry.

An inspector was always trained, tested, and certified throughout their career on a monthly, quarterly, and yearly basis. This was accomplished through monthly meeting with training seminars, quarterly you would be reviewed by your supervisor, and every three years you would have to be certified by having a supervisor accompany you through three or four days inspections.

It would always please me to have a supervisor come along on the exercises because I found that they were kept in the office to long and sometimes lost touch with the industry as well as the inspection process outside of the training seminars. It happened on of my last certification trips and the food service supervisor for the district accompanied me to a restaurant in my area. This was quite away from his district office and he was enjoying the day.

The restaurant was not in bad shape and the owners prided themselves on the cleanliness of their establishment. I found the hood vents to be installed improperly but more serious was the operation of their dishwashing machine. It was one of the one armed bandits as we used to call them. It was chemical supplied with chlorine sanitizer, soap, and rinse additive to make the dishes shine and air-dry faster.

I showed the operator of the restaurant how dull his silverware was and he should have noticed immediately that something was wrong. He said he had called the service man from the company they buy their chemical from, but they would not be able to send him out to address the problem until later in the week. This was not at all acceptable.

I drew from my many years of working with dishwashing machines in my past and surmised the problem. The chemicals were all in five gallon buckets with colored coated tubes running into the top of each bucket. The buckets were color coated as well with labels to distinguish what the product was inside. The chlorine was supposed to be a yellow tube, the soap was to be a blue tube, and the fast drying additive was a red tube. These were to match the Yellow label on the chlorine, the blue label on the soap, and the red label on the additive.

A quick look and it was obvious the tubes were not in the proper containers. I brought the operator to the dishwasher machine and arranged the tubes properly. We ran the machine two or three times and the chemical tested properly using chlorine strips. Everybody was happy as all the violations were corrected on the hood filters and the dish machine.

When the inspection was over and we went out to the car after the inspection the supervisor asked me how I knew what the problem with the machine was and how did I know how to correct it. I just said experience and the will to work with the industry.

While we are on the subject of test strips for checking sanitized solutions I would like to cover the types of strips we would use. One was for chlorine, one was quaternary ammonia, and the third was iodine, which was acceptable under the regulations for sanitize solutions to be used for dishwashing machine, three compartment sinks, and wiping cloths.

Now in my early days as an inspector for the Division of Hotels and Restaurants I had the unfortunate accident of burning my right hand severally. The rehabilitation was soaking my hand in iodine until it was discovered that I was highly allergic to iodine. I had broken out with blisters from my head to my toes and it took six weeks of therapy to overcome the problem. I was then instructed to never touch or consume even iodine salt or I would have the same reaction.

Consequently, I would always ask the manager or operator of an iodine operated dishwashing machine, three compartments sink, bar sink, or sanitize station for wiping cloths to test the product with the iodine strips. Again, working with the industry.

One of the areas that needed constant assistance from the inspector but little was granted by the district offices was in the area of helping a new owner to get open. It was considered an information call and inspectors were to be inspecting hotels, apartments, or restaurants with little or no time rendered for information calls. Later in the years I spent with the department an 800-telephone number was given to the industry to answer any of their questions. Unfortunately, they would refer to the number as the number from Hell, as they were left on hold or left waiting for hours before it was answered.

Most inspectors that I discussed the problem with would squeeze in the information calls and answer to their supervisors later about their time spent outside of the inspections.

It happened that I got myself in all kinds of trouble trying to help a Greek fellow trying to open his business in a food court at a Mall. He had almost finished his construction and a order came down from Tallahassee that all food prep areas in an establishment would have to have bathroom facilities for their employees. If they could not accomplish this task a variance would have to be issued by the office of review in Tallahassee. This review board would meet only once a month and all other request for a variance would have to wait for the next meeting. This order was a rule made up by a new leader in the department in Tallahassee.

The Greek restaurant owner had paid two months rent in advance to the Mall management and his bathroom facilities for employees and customers were the gang toilet adjacent to the food court. The department took the stand that there would be no exceptions to their rule. This meant that the restaurant owner would have to pay another months rent and still not open for business. The restaurant owner was not only being squeezed by the landlord for another months rent but also, the department that wanted a three hundred dollar fee for a variance.

After asking the department to understand that the food courts in the Mall were the same throughout the state and the food prep areas were never designed to accommodate restrooms. The department would not budge and I let the owner know their decision. I wrestled with this problem for the rest of the day and decided to try and help the industry.

I made a call to my local state congressman and explained the situation. He immediately entered the leader's office in Tallahassee and asked what he was trying to do to our businessmen in the state.

I immediately received a phone call from my district office and was told to bring all my state equipment, car, and documents to the office by the end of the week.

I then made a call back to my congressman and relayed the information I had received. His response was: where and when?

That Friday, my congressman arrived at the district office before me and stated he wanted to be there to see the inspector receive his award for helping the industry. The district office was busy tearing up the dismissal papers and scurrying around the office explaining the inspector has a congressman to represent him.

The result was a verbal reprimand issued by my district supervisor and the leader in Tallahassee was later suspended for prior offenses in a hiring discrimination case. Future variances were disbanded. I felt again that I had worked with the industry.

CHAPTER 22

SURPRISE!

The 24 years I spent going in and out of restaurants and hotels there was bound to be a few surprises. The beginning of each day was always an adventure because it was always something new or at new locations.

This day was to start as so many others over the 24 years. I awoke with the Florida morning sunshine glistening from the East breaking through my bedroom window. They said it was going to be a scorcher today with the temperature in the 80s. This did not scare this northerner from being up to the challenge. I had graduated on a day when the temperature was minus 52 degrees. So, bring on the hot weather and I was looking forward to a beautiful day.

Usually, I left the house at 7:30 a.m. and headed for my usual stop. It was a place called Finlandia Bakery where I would have my first cup of coffee and greet a lot of fellow coffee hounds. We would tackle the local gossip and solve the morning word puzzle game in the local newspaper. We were always looking forward to Elvie Anttilla's latest bakery sweet and most would be off to work or for the retirees another cup of cover and a little cardamon bread.

It would be 8 or 8:15 by the time I headed south to Rivera Beach. Each evening I would plan my stops for the next day and it was possible to complete at least ten inspections, half being restaurants and half being lodgings. Today was going to be an easy day of inspections because the weather was beautiful, the coffee great, and the cardimon bread especially sweet.

As I headed down U.S. highway 1 out of Stuart, I noticed the seasonal traffic had departed for the North and traffic was moving a lot faster. Driving past Cove Road and past the Country Clubs where traffic was usually lined up to leave the Clubs and enter onto the highway, I found very little travelers. The ride was going to be very pleasant, just like the rest of the day.

There went the entrance to Lost Lake where the Clubhouse kitchen was run by an all girl staff. Every time they hired a male to work in the kitchen he was dismissed as goofing off or inadequate from dishwashing to cooking. The girls kept the most perfect kitchen and even the baker's area was found spotless and that is really something considering bakers were usually covered with flour. One time I found a violation in there kitchen because the baker forgot to label her container she put in the walk-in. She immediately grabbed it out of my hands and proceeded to brand the product. They were all very upset that they had received a violation and dismissed me as a male intruder in their world.

I remember the ladies had planned a summer vacation all together in a motor home to cruise the West and they were going to call it the Thelma and Louise Getaway.

It was a brilliant sunny day without a cloud in the sky as the sun was still rising over the left side of my car. I noticed the Mariner Sands Country Club one of the oldest establishments in the area. They still kept up the grounds and I really appreciated the respect and consideration they had for me as their inspector. They would always contact me if they were going to do a remodel of their dining facilities and asked for my opinion or advice. It was always a pleasure working with them. They were always very professional.

Now I could relax, as there was quite a distance of open space before I came to Hobe Sound area. I would pass the old room 999 on my left at the Palms Motel and Suites and come up on Bridge Road at the only traffic light in town. There was Harry and the Natives on my right but no time to stop and up the rise to cross the tracks and on to the tangled trees lining the road. This was the area of the Johnathan Dickinson State Park, which I will talk about in a later chapter. I had to be careful around here because sometimes an occasional deer will dart out on the road and cross over for no apparent reason.

I pushed forward to slow down entering Palm Beach County where it is 45 miles per hour and strictly enforced by the Tequesta Police Department. The town is the entryway to Jupiter and I will have to make up my mind as to staying on U.S. 1 or taking a slight detour onto A1A that follows the coast. The weather being as it was there was no hesitation as I turned to the left at the traffic light beyond the inlet bridge and the Jupiter lighthouse back on my left.

I thought to myself, it was such a beautiful day and somebody had to travel to work on such a day so why not make the best of it. The parasail surfboarders were already high in the sky over the water, the joggers were running on the sidewalks, and the skateboards were swerving and gliding down the bike path avoiding their bike mates along beside the road. It was only 35 miles per hour and why would anyone want to go any faster and miss all these sights.

I met a young lady who was biking on the very same sidewalk and she tried to go off to the bike path but lost her balance and fell. She felt pretty stupid and ended up with a bruised eye and a cut on her lip. Everyone came to her rescue and even Paramedics were called to the scene. I would always kid her that she was the only biker I knew that should have gotten a BWI because she admitted to having a little brew before biking.

After the stop sign at Donald Ross Road and the end of the beach tour, I had to pass through Juno Beach. This was a beautiful little town full of condos on the ocean and a city hall beside a little lake surrounded by a walkway. On my right was the castle belonging to a builder that I had remodel a dining room in my home. It is a real castle and he always said a man's home is his castle.

Now it was time to come back to reality and at the light was U.S. 1. Here I made my left and passed Seminole Country Club, the oldest on the East coast of Florida, and proceeded to North Palm Beach, Lake Park, and then arriving in Rivera Beach.

There had been quite a bit of controversy as of late in Rivera Beach concerning vagrants or homeless people breaking into restaurants in the evening. It was not taken to seriously because there was little damage and the trespasser seemed to be only interested in cooking him a meal and then leaving. The worst scenario found a broken lock or a door window broken so he could gain access to the establishment. The restaurants were on the lower scale dining facilities, staying away from the fast food places, or the fine dining places.

So, here I had arrived and my very first stop on this beautiful sunny warm Florida day was at a little ten seat diner place nestled behind a gas station on the corner of Blue Heron Blvd. and U.S. 1. The name escapes my now but no matter, I was shocked to find three Rivera Beach Police cars and the local fire department truck parked out in front of the establishment taking up almost the entire parking lot. I approached the entrance that was all taped off by yellow no trespassing ribbon and produced my identification as I ducked under the tape.

An officer recognized me and stated you won't believe this but the midnight diner has struck again and it looks like his last meal. I looked into the diner and there stood the owner alongside the chief of police. The owner was almost in tears and I looked at the grill area behind the counter and saw the fire department personnel struggling to extract a pair of legs from the hood system. It seems the midnight diner has tried to enter the establishment through the hood system, got lodged by the narrow space, sheet metal screws catching him, and had kicked the gas line trying to get free, thereby fixating himself.

This was not how this beautiful day was to begin but I later found out the owner could not see himself cooking on that grill ever again and he sold the restaurant within the month.

I deserved to have a couple of easy inspections after that and I finished a pizza parlor, a hot dog wagon, a coffee shop and a hotel kitchen. After inspecting the hotel lodging rooms I was ready for a lunch break. But, thinking about that poor midnight diner I could only muster a glass of soda.

Later that afternoon I went to my other scheduled stops and finally was looking forward to my final stop. It was located directly behind the Riviera Police Department building and was a quick little take out diner. As I pulled up to the street to the location, I noticed a car with the trunk open. Two other cars were backing up to them and I found myself having to go around them to get to the parking area in front of the restaurant I wanted to insect.

Next thing I hear is all these police sirens and men yelling at the top of their voices to get down and out of your cars. I just stopped my car dead in the street. Police cars surrounded my car and an officer asked me to roll down my window and told me to leave the area now by backing up and come back later. No problem!

Now, I was about to give up the rest of the day's assignment, but by an hour later the mess was cleaned up and I completed the inspection. The owner informed me that the drug dealers were so brazen with their business they thought that right behind the Police headquarters was the safest place in town. Wrong again and the owner was very happy to see the area cleaned up for a change.

The return to home was on I-95 and I was anxious to enjoy a nice quite time in Martin County where they have a county slogan, "Come Enjoy Our Better Nature!" I was ready for that.

CHAPTER 23

THE PLANET CITIES

I called them the planet cities because they are named Jupiter and Juno. The closest town was Jupiter and I always enjoyed traveling to the coastal town with its inlet and its famous lighthouse that overlooks the busy traffic of fishing boats, leisure yachts, and occasional tour sightseeing boats. Across the inlet there are several fine restaurants with leisurely dining atmosphere as the patrons enjoy the inlet traffic.

There was one occasion I scheduled to inspect the Crab House as it was called back then and I was deep into my kitchen routine when all hell broke loose in the back of the establishment. It seems there was a new delivery driver backing into the loading dock and he was not aware of a sprinkler line that his truck caught and brought the entire system down spewing water throughout the kitchen. I was deeply engrossed with the working of the automatic dishwasher that was continuously out of chemical.

Needless to say, I understood their plight and rescheduled for a dryer day to complete their inspection.

All hands were on deck with a mop in their hand and water gushing out everywhere. I knew that on my return visit every corner of that kitchen should be pretty spotless.

To the West of the Crab House was the Jetty Restaurant that was owned by a Michigan family and they also owned a fine dining restaurant in Juno. I will always remember giving them their opening inspection in November of that year and I was surprised to see them busy decorating a Christmas tree in the front entrance. I quarried why now and they said we hope to be to busy in December to have time for the tree. They were fine restaurant people and knew what they were talking about. The place was always busy and I could never forget when I took a friend there for dinner. A Jamaican band was entertaining us and the bandleader came to our table to introduce himself as an owner of a restaurant in Rivera Beach. I did recognize him and he played some special numbers just for us.

Jupiter had many interesting places with Burt Reynolds dinner theater, his Back Stage restaurant, and out west of town he had a restaurant at his old family farm and petting zoo. All these have changed hands now and are not operating under Burt Reynolds name. Mr. Reynolds was always a celebrity in Jupiter and never passed up an opportunity to welcome a new business in town with his visit and best wishes on a signed photo of himself.

One particular location was a place called Judy's Highway Café. It was strictly a biker's bar with bumpers across the parking lot that read bikers only. The owner Judy and Victor had put up a lot of actors on bikes from their movies like Steve McQueen in the Great Escape and Marlon Brando from Hells Angels. Now, Judy and Victor were from Germany and Judy had returned to her hometown after many year abroad and opened the bar with many different beers and a home for all the motorcyclists in the area. So one day in walks Burt Reynolds. He looks around and asks big heavyset Victor behind the bar, "Where's my picture"!

Victor with his native German accent replies, "So, who the hell are you"!

Immediately, Burt was taken back and explained who he was and welcomed the new owners to the area. He promised to bring in some pictures and sure enough they were from the movie Best Little Whore House in Texas, the German version. His signature was there of course and his best wishes.

Back in Jupiter I loved to inspect the Jupiter Bridge Restaurant with its horseshoe counter, plastic covered bench booths, and atmosphere of the old Walgreen's lunch counter. The establishment changed hands many times and I would say the best were a couple of Scandinavian bakers that made the place busy and profitable. They were constantly being harassed by local ordinances regarding their sign and they finally tired of the problems and retired. I believe the business is no longer operating.

Turning left at the traffic light before you cross the Jupiter inlet bridge would take you out on the Jupiter

Island where mega rich folks live and their clubhouse, hotel, and cottages. This is worth another chapter by itself later. Turning right at the same light will take us on A1A and to the intersection of Indiantown Road where there is a shopping center on your left. Here is the Royal Café eatery that gave me much pleasure as an inspector. The owners ran a very successful operation due to very hard work and a fantastic staff. I always found the owner and his wife in attendance and looking after their patrons who returned every day. I never had a problem until one day I broke the cardinal rule of introduction. Sometimes you get to familiar with a staff and proceed with the inspection prior to speaking to the owner. So, out of the kitchen he came and confronted me as to who gave me permission to go behind the counter. I was so surprised by his reaction I had to apologize all over the place. The girls recognized me and said to go ahead, but I should have waited to see the owner. Later, he apologized to me saying he was going over the sales of the previous day and was a bit upset. Unfortunately, I received his wrath but was warranted, as I did not follow procedure. The Royal Café has changed ownership and I cannot speak of its present standings.

To the East of this intersection on Indiantown Road there is a Duffy's Restaurant and on the West end of town on the same street is another Duffy's Restaurant just before you cross over I-95. They were both opened and operated by a single investor as a sport bar and grill.

The chain grew so fast and was so well accepted by the sport minded clientele throughout south Florida that eventually the entire franchise was bought out by a corporation. The earlier days of its development was exciting because the original owner would call on me to consult with him on changes or ask for my advice on several ideas.

I liked that a lot and helped them to find several locations to expand their operations when I heard of a restaurant going out of business. No compensation was expected or received other than the satisfaction of knowing another good restaurant was going to open and be successful.

One of my favorite restaurant operations in Jupiter was the Miller's Ale House. This operation was also a sports bar and grill. It was always busy and scheduling inspections was very uncomfortable because the cooking area was very close and you had to work your way around and behind cooks while the place was open. They did keep things in order and temperatures were always maintained with very little exceptions. Jack Miller the owner was on the staff all the time to stay on top of everything and when equipment started to fail he was there to see it was replaced with the newest available units. Jack Miller gave his inspectors a lot of respect and the inspectors respected him as well. Unfortunately in his later years Mr. Miller started loosing his eyesight and he had to delicate a lot of his responsibilities. I miss him a lot and wish him well.

Out to the West on Indiantown Road there was a shopping center on the south side of the road where I met some Polish people opening a new deli with mostly takeout service. Being that I was still married to a Polish lady I kind of took a special interest in their efforts to operate a good deli.

One day, Mrs. Lapinski asked me if I could help her daughter get a job with the State of Florida as a health inspector. I had met her daughter in the deli and she seemed very nice, young, and not afraid of hard work. I asked Mrs. Lapinski if her daughter had a college degree as required by the department. She already had the experience of working in the food service industry obviously. Mrs. Lapinski stated she had a Bachelor of Science in business from Florida State. I asked what was the problem with her not being able to find a job.

Mrs. Lapinski said the problem was her name and every time her daughter would fill out an application and go for an interview the interviewer would not stop laughing. She was left out of the job market because of her name. This was during the President Clinton years and the young girl's name was Monica Lapinski. Not Lawinsi thank God.

I told them I would talk to my District Director and give her a recommendation and arrange for an interview after she filled out the application. Two weeks later I was training Monica and she became one of our best inspectors ever. About two years later Monica asked for an administrative leave so she could go back and get her Masters degree.

Happily she completed the work and met a nice young man to marry, changed her last name, and moved to Utah.

Back East down Indiantown Road when you meet U.S. 1 I would make a left turn and head South to the corner of Donald Ross Road and U.S. 1. Here I would remember back when I was in my twenties and managed a Howard Johnson Restaurant on this very corner. I can never forget the day the termites decided to swarm right during the lunch rush. The pests came out of the walls under the glass windows all across the front of the dining room. Every customer was covered with the flying insects, as well as all their meals on the table of booths that lined the dining area. Everyone just started screaming and headed for the door. The manager, that was I, was yelling, "Don't worry, everything is on the house! We will be closed for a few days! Please come back after the tent has been removed"!

Now it is a Seafood Restaurant but had a very bad opening prior to the present owners. The place was completely remodeled with a lot of inlaid tile work on the entrance and walls. I was the inspector that arrived for their opening inspection and found them to be in compliance with everything except one detail. They had to seal the holes in the storage closet that opened to the parking lot out back. They did not know that I had a history with the place and were surprised when I showed them the problem. The following day I approved their operation and they were open for business.

They were very good cooks and management looked after the place like it was their only life. Unfortunately, they had an incident that caused the restaurant to close within six months. Now, their dishes were quite spicy but customers where warned and could order them without the spices. But, one day a customer called from the emergency room of Jupiter Hospital to say that he was sick from their food. Another call came to the restaurant and then another. A panic set in with the owner and he called of all people the local TV station.

The next day after the broadcast there were over one hundred calls to the health department and the State Hotels and Restaurants division. Some callers could not even tell the inspectors where the restaurant was located but the complaints knew they had eaten there. The final story was an angry employee that was fired had put a chemical into the ice machine and anyone who drank a glass of ice water had a reaction to the chemical.

The restaurant could not recover and went out of business.

This was the town of Juno. Across the street on Donald Ross Road was the second restaurant called the Reef that was owned by the same people that owned the Jetty Restaurant on the Jupiter Inlet. The Reef was a high scale fine dining establishment that was very professionally run. The staff was always well trained, certified, and dressed for the occasion of serving fine foods, spirits, and hospitality. It is always a task to point out that no matter the class of restaurant the bartenders will still mix the ice chilling the bottles of wine with the ice that they put into glasses. They will also skip the ice scoop during a busy time to dip the glass into the ice bin and create a violation of sanitary conditions as the bottles are contaminated and the glass can be broken in the ice.

The town of Juno had two other establishments on the south end of town that was known for their seafood. The oldest being the Captains Table and the other was a porch and quick luncheon style restaurant. The Captains Table had a fine reputation and the staff was well trained. The other establishment had a turn over of staff and was always struggling to make ends meet. When an establishment has such a turnover of help the training and certifications are always a problem.

The last establishment I can cover was that of the Florida Power and Light headquarters that had a very large kitchen to feed their staff. It was a big cafeteria-style establishment and a very large kitchen staff that was trained very well. The biggest problem with this establishment was the security and trying to get in to do an inspection. I was always detained at the security point of entry and I felt that it was because the kitchen was being prepared for an inspection.

The drive back to my home in Martin County was always a pleasure as I would take the A1A route along the Atlantic and watch the kite surfers, bikers, joggers, and skateboarders along the way. Of course you had to look out for the bikini-clad bathers, as they would cross the street to get to the beach or back to their cars in the parking lot. I would always remind myself that this was a tough job but somebody had to do it. Why not me!

CHAPTER 24

A RESORT HOTEL

"A tangy Tuesday"! I heard Jennifer Ross explain on my radio. It was 7:00 o'clock in the morning and the radio came on right on time. I was always thankful to hear Jennifer's voice in the morning. I would kid everyone at work that I had a perky beautiful girl waking me up which was just to bolster my ego as I found myself single and out of the dating game for awhile.

I met Jennifer Ross once when I was assigned to cover the food vendors at a hot air balloon event in Royal Palm Beach. It was held at the golf course and she was setting up for the coverage by the local radio station. She was running around carrying a Corona and complaining that she partied too much the night before. She was hot and had the cutest figure for a 20 something girl. We talked briefly and I was off to inspect the temporary event food vendors. Unfortunately, I would only hear her voice each morning to brighten my day.

It was a Tuesday and I was looking forward to the day ahead. I had planned to spend the entire day in Palm Beach. The inspection sheets had been prepared with the titles, addresses, and occupancy for all the locations in the Palm Beach resort. They had seven kitchens and three lodging license locations. So the day was going to be extremely busy but pleasurable.

The drive from my residence in Lake Worth was not to far but the traffic was unusually busy. I would drive North on U.S. 1 to avoid the heavier traffic on I-95. Turning right on Southern Blvd and north again on Olive would take me all the way down to Okeechobee Blvd. Turning east on Okeechobee Blvd. with the Palm Beach University behind me I crossed the Royal Palm Way bridge just in time to see the red traffic light come on and the crossbar come down. The traffic all came to a stop and I had time to enjoy the beautiful Intracoastal Waterway. Then a gleaming white luxury liner with its black windows along the first deck passed under the bridge and the bridge started to close and the crossbars went up.

It was nice to be the first car to cross because the Royal Palm trees lined both sides of the road and median were a spectacular and wonderful greeting to the island of Palm Beach. I passed the Palm Beach Academy School I had the pleasure of inspecting as a county inspector. Now, as a State health inspector I only inspected and licensed public food service and lodging establishments.

Onward to the East, passing the statue of Elish Newton Dimick, Legislator, developer and friend the plaque reads; I traveled until I came to the South County Road. I took a left and passed the magnificent

Presbyterian Church on my right where many notable wealthy people attended and many marriages where held (the latest being Michael Jordan). Next came the South entrance to a Resort Hotel and finally the main entrance to the right. I was greeted about half way down by a security guard, at their hut in the middle of the street. They asked why I was there and I showed my identification letting them know that I was there to inspect the hotel and the food service. The guard pointed toward the hotel and told me to park on the left side of fountain that fronted the entrance to the lobby.

I took the circle around the fountain that had two levels of water pouring over its edges to flood a base. It was full of coins from wishes tossed by guests hoping to return to this beautiful resort. The parking lot was not to full and I was able to find a place very close to the entrance. Getting all my stuff together from the trunk and making sure I would not have to return to my car before the inspection was over; I proceeded to walk toward the entrance.

I had to pass the valet personnel that were rushing frantically to return cars or park cars for the guests. They were all very neatly dressed in white shirts, clean-shaven, sporting kaki shorts, and white tennis shoes. They were greeting the guests and politely thanking them for gratuities or welcoming them to the resort.

The doorman was standing at one of the entry doors and I chose the center door as he held it open and welcomed me to the resort. Once inside I immediately walked toward the concierge's desk to the left and again showed my identification and introduced myself to a sharply dressed young lady in a blue blazer suit. She picked up a phone and called the assistant manger of the hotel. While I awaited her arrival I asked how the season was going and mentioned how I appreciated their attention.

I must regress to my entrance into the lobby area of the resort hotel. One cannot avoid raising their eyes upward to the magnificent forty-foot high ceiling. It is very difficult to avoid stopping to admire the columns lining both sides of the lobby that rise to support the beautiful maidens painted at the top. Each maiden is adorned with a different pose, either carrying a water urn or supporting a palm fan, or ready to sooth you with a massage at the spa.

The ceiling has arches that meet surrounding painted murals of a maiden riding a horse or a greek god and his three horses. The ceiling is painted in gold with beautiful colors to take your breath away. If you are stopped long enough to take this all in the first time you are probably going to be run over by other tourists or staff members trying to make their way to their designated appointments.

The hotel assistant manager, who I have had the pleasure of meeting before on my inspections, met me at the concierge's desk. She was always so impressive, showing a stature of authority, professionally dressed in a blue-blazer with matching skirt, and immediately demanding the presence of the staff to escort us through the inspection process.

Within less than five minutes a staff had met the assistant manager and myself, all carrying two-way-radio's or pocket recorders. The head of maintenance was present as well as the food and beverage manager, the head of housekeeping, and a member of the office of operations. I had to explain to them that all of them were not needed at one time as I had to inspect the front desk and pick out at least a half dozen rooms to go through. We would return to the lobby within an hour and proceed to the kitchens.

This was unfortunate but necessary and allowed the kitchen staff to be alerted ahead of time to have the place ship shape within the hour. It was not a worry on my part because the food service operation is so large that one-hour would not make a big deal of difference. The food and beverage manger left and the others waited for me to finish the necessary tasks to be completed behind the front desk.

The front desk was manned by very polite well dressed staff members and were usually very busy helping guests to check-in or out of the resort hotel. They were all very cordial, making sure the guests were well informed of their experience and opportunities at the hotel. I had to part one of the desk staff members to let me pull past reservations of previous guests to verify the charges in accordance with the posted rates displayed at the desk. All was in order and then I found six rooms at different locations throughout the hotel on a random basis. This would give me a good idea of the standards that were to be met by the State of Florida.

The assistant managers then guided me to the elevators as the operations staff member, the head of housekeeping, and the head of maintenance followed close behind. Once on the elevator and the doors closed, I immediately reached for the telephone and picked it up to see that an emergency operator answered. I explained I was just testing the line. I verified the existence of an elevator license and that it was current. The elevator came to a smooth stop at the sixth floor and we exited all together.

The head of housekeeping unlocked the first room with her passkey and she announced our entry into the room. The room was empty and ready to be inspected. I approached the head of the bed and let my hand reach under the bedspread. A quick throw from my arm left the bed spread at the foot of the bed and the sheet exposed. There were no hairs, stains, spots, and the top sheet was pulled back to show the bottom sheet was just as spotless. The bed was made with the trained staff leaving folded corners, turned borders at the top under the pillows, and all the bedding was in order with the proper thread count and expected from a five-star hotel.

I then looked under the bed to observe whether the floor was being vacuumed thoroughly and there was no debris left behind from previous guests. So far so good, and as I got up from the floor, I noticed a burn spot on the carpet by the headboard. It was a cigarette burn and the maintenance director immediately spoke to his recorder to have it repaired giving the room number and location.

Next I proceeded to the restroom and pulled the stopper from the sink. There was not hair present and I turned the water valves on to check for hot water and leaks once the valves were closed. The shower curtain was clean without any water or soap spots, and the shower stall was shining after the thorough cleaning by the staff.

The lock on the door was sufficient with a secondary lock and complete with a deadbolt. The rate sheet and Florida laws were posted on the door with the check out time present. A quick look through the drawers, the closet, and the operation of the television, I was satisfied that the room met the requirements of the Florida State Laws governing the operations of a hotel.

This inspection continued for the other five rooms I had selected and they were all found to be in compliance with the exceptions of one or two minor violations that were noted on the inspection report. The violations were immediately either corrected on the spot or recorded on their equipment to be corrected as soon as possible.

The smoke detectors were all tested and passed in each room and the hearing impaired units had been tested behind the front desk before we had started inspecting the rooms.

We then proceeded to the laundry area of the hotel and I inspected for fire hazards, fire equipment available and up to date with inspection tags. The laundry was massive and people were very busy completing their assigned duties in the laundry. Everything was orderly and clean. I especially checked the dryers to make sure the lint traps were being cleaned regularly and that no excess lint was allowed to buildup, which could cause a fire hazard.

I thanked the head of housekeeping and complimented her and the staff for a job well done. I expected the few shortcomings would be corrected and excused her from our inspection process.

Now we would proceed to the foodservice areas and join up with the food and beverage manager. The staff member from operations, the head of maintenance, as well as the assistant manager entered a small hallway off from the lobby that led to the first station.

We passed by the administrative office and made a right turn into an area known as the room service center. Here there were multiple operations going on. A room was set up with silverware burnishing machines and the silverware was in many different stages of being cleaned and stored. It is always a concern that silverware and utensils are handled properly to avoid hand contact with the eating portion at all times. When silverware is stored properly the handles are always toward the server.

The room service room was stocked with all the necessary items from carts, linens, glasses, salt and peppershakers, and beverages. All these items were to be in excellent condition and any needed service or repair were to be immediately removed from service. The room had immediate access to the elevators and was located just steps from the kitchen prep area. The food brought into the room service area is kept under a stainless steel cover until it arrives at the room that is requested the service.

There are so many details an inspector must be on the alert to make sure that all items sent to a room is not reused until it is completely cleaned and sanitized. All individual items like butter, creamers, jelly cups, etc. are to be used one time and then discarded. Carts must be wiped down with disinfectants and sanitizers.

Stepping down to the food prep area and the main kitchen, to the right was a raised office area. This was the office of the head chef, in charge of all the kitchens at the resort hotel. He was a robust gentleman that wore the tallest hat in the establishment. He commanded the entire respect from everyone around him. He had the knowledge of every employee within his realm and he was the first I had to speak to about the information I needed for a complete inspection.

First was a list of all of his employees, their required food safety training completion and those scheduled to be trained in the food safety courses. Food Managers training had to be recorded and their cards produced by each kitchen mangers having the card in their possession. The head chef had all his paper work in order and then welcomed us to inspect his kitchens.

My first concern was to observe the kitchen staff members as they were preparing food items. The personnel had to be wearing gloves during the handling of raw foods. The foods must never be contaminated, by handling different types of food such as chicken and then beef. Staff should change gloves or wash hands whenever possible to make sure contamination does not occur. The hand sinks were located properly and used continuously or else a violation was noted.

When I first came to the resort hotel, their kitchen was in a transition from a very old system of gutters below all their pipes surrounding the walls of the kitchen. It was quite a sight to behold, as this would stop any leaking pipes from dropping onto the floor area. Now the pipes were completely out of sight and stainless steel ceiling panels covered the entire area.

The equipment was continuously being replaced with new and modern equipment. Many times I would have to stop and ask how this piece of equipment was working. But, still the most important pieces of equipment were inspected like meatslicers, can openers, wire whips, and dishmachines.

Meatslicers were to be cleaned each time a different product was used on it and I also was aware of the slicers causing the greatest number of personnel accidents if not cleaned properly.

With my years of experience in the food service industry I was always eager to suggest having wet terrycloth be placed over the blade while the meatslicer was being cleaned. Thereby protecting the cleaner from being cut by the blade. It was always a sure bet you would see a food service employee with a finger cut off or a glove covering a bandaged hand. If the wound were severe enough the employee would be removed from the kitchen.

An inspector felt a since of accomplishment in the duration of inspecting a food service facility when he witnessed improvements.

At first, while walking through the resort kitchen, I would find wooden spoons that were worn to a frazil, wooden bowls used for serving salads and fruit, and an old butcher-block table scored and grooved due to continuous usage. These items were considered a violation of wooden utensils not authorized for use in commercial food service. The spoons would retain bacteria after they had been cracked or worn on the edges. The bowls would loose their finish and become storage breading grounds for bacteria. The butcher-block table had to be maintained by cutting the service completely level and finished to prevent bacteria from growing on its service. A good butcher-block is best maintained daily or better to be covered with a synthetic cutting board.

While walking through the kitchen I could see such great improvement in the results of the staff listening to my advice and their utensils were all made of approved food grade materials. They were appreciative of my suggestions and always explaining to them the reasons why instead of just quoting the law.

Metal whips were always a source of violation when a wire was broken and hanging from the handle. I would explain that the whip was not useless but could still be operational if the wire was broken off from the handle on the other end. I also recommended a trick I had learned from previous experiences in the food industry.

The wire could be bent into a hook and used to store the shellfish tags for ninety days as required by law. Many of the food service establishments that I had inspected used the idea.

The dishwashing machine in the main kitchen was a high temperature conveyor unit. The dishes were set on a conveyor system where the dishware was exposed to high-pressure water spray and went through three cycles of wash, rinse, and sanitize. The dishes came out clean, shiny, and dry to the touch. They were then stacked on racks to be transported to the service areas. It was noted that on the evening shifts at the restaurant during the week all of the stainless steel ceiling panels were sent through this machine.

Leaving the main kitchen area the entourage moved to a large bar area serving a circular room and ballrooms down the north hallway.

All bartenders have a bad habit of storing wine bottles to be chilled in the same ice bin used to serve ice in the drinks. This is not permitted because the bottles are never cleaned and the ice becomes contaminated. The bartenders at the resort hotel did not have this problem because a bin was provided for just the chilling of the bottles.

This resort hotel is very well known for their Sunday Brunch where your wine glass will never be empty. It is a spectacular event that should be experienced at least once in your life. The buffet is complete with chefs to prepare your omelet, poached eggs, Belgium waffle, or whatever kind of breakfast you would like. The tables are centered with ice carvings of unimaginable figures from swans to dolphins. The dishes surrounding the endless tables have food fit for a king. Breakfast is featured at one end of the table that curves around to another end that provides you with shrimp, lobster, king crab claws, beef, pork, chicken, turkey, lamb, lasagna, spaghetti, Swedish meatballs, endless numbers of fresh vegetables, and a dessert ensemble of cakes, pastry, ice cream, soufflés, and countless other decadent temptations.

All the while you are trying to make up your mind as to which entry you wish to start with, a harpist is playing wonderful music that fills the room. It is all very impressive and a bit expensive. When I first came to this resort hotel the price was sixty-five dollars in the 80"s. Recently, I asked some young hostess's and they quoted a price now of ninety-five dollars.

It was in the 80's that I decided to take my Mother to the grand party and it was on her birthday. The hotel was doing some renovating in the circular room so the event was moved to another dining room on the south side of the hotel. It was grand and we were warmly greeted at our table by first the resort hotel Asst. Manager, then the Head Chef with his very high chefs hat, and then the harpist. Finally, my Mother said she became embarrassed with all the attention. I told her, "Mom, don't worry. The other guests will just think you are a wealthy Palm Beach lady out to lunch with her pool man"! We laughed our way through lunch and I will always cherish the memory as my mother passed away before her next birthday.

The second time I attended the resort hotel Sunday Brunch was for my twentieth anniversary to my lovely wife. At this occasion we invited my brother and his wife, to join us. This time the brunch was held in the circular room. Again the food and experience was wonderful. A most memorable moment was when my brother was shocked to see the gentleman and his young dining companion leave a one hundred dollar bill on the table for a gratuity.

The inspection was not even half over and we went down the North hallway beautifully decorated with chandeliers and exquisite furniture. Looking up at the lighted ceiling with rays up each supporting column you must be careful not to loose your step. The group continued on to the east toward the Atlantic ocean. We passed a conference room, a ball room, and a banquet room before the large windows looking out at the ocean at the end of the hallway. We crossed the ball boom opening the fifteen-foot tall double doors to enter the South hallway. Here we entered a kitchen known as the Banquet Kitchen. It had several very large cookers that were made for cooking recipes to accommodate the large number of guests attending banquets. The cookers were always left very clean and I would inspect the openings for any product left behind. They were always spotless. Utensils were found lining the rack suspended from the ceiling over the grills and ovens. All was in order and the Banquet Kitchens passed with very few exceptions.

The inspection of the kitchens also included the hood systems, fire equipment (like fire extinguishers, hoses, and alarm). The State health inspectors were trained and considered Special Fire Inspectors while I served for the State of Florida. To this day I cannot pass a fire extinguisher without looking at its tag to see if it is current and the needle on the unit is in the upright position. It is just a habit that will probably never leave me.

Leaving the Banquet Kitchen we made our way back down the South hallway to the elevator leading to the basement. There we would find the kitchen for employee meals, staffed with the same well-dressed kitchen personnel. They wore white smoges with black pants and a white chefs hat. Runners to carry the food to the serving line wore checkered black and white jackets with black pants. Every employee wore very clean black shoes.

In front of the kitchen was a self-serve line where the employees helped themselves to the special for the day adding beverages and dessert on a tray you carried to a friendly dining room. The atmosphere was bright and cheerful with soft music surrounding their break room. Bulletin boards noted the wage and hour laws and schedules for food service training. There were other events posted for the employees to participate during their free time.

The kitchen for employee dining did have its importance as it assured the continuous healthfulness of service to the resort hotel. Only, healthy foods were prepared for all of them.

After a quick lunch break, I insisted on paying for mine, we headed for the Ocean Bar. This was one of my favorite stops because it had such a fantastic view of the Atlantic and a forty-foot aquarium bar top. The tropical fish swimming by as you sat to have a meal and drinks was quite relaxing. The kitchen at the north end of the bar dining area was well exposed and you could watch the staff preparing your food. The establishment was quite cramped but kept very orderly and passed without any major violation.

There are so many duties for an inspector, while inspecting a food service establishment beyond all those I have already mentioned. One of the most important is taking temperatures. Cold food must be kept cold and hot foods kept hot. Cold foods are to be kept at 41degrees or colder and hot foods at 140 degrees or hotter. Walk-ins, and reach-ins, steam tables, as well as holding boxes have to be checked. Inspectors must calibrate their thermometers before starting the inspection and ask the staff to join him as they calibrate theirs.

The calibration is done with a glass of ice and dipping the probe thermometer into the ice. The dial on the thermometer face can read 32 degrees and adjusted by turning the nut on the bottom of the face. Alcohol swabs will be used during the testing of temperatures to wipe the probe of the thermometer each time it is used. The supply of swabs is endless and an inspection is not complete or correct unless all temperatures are noted and recorded on the inspection sheet.

Litmus papers are used to test the chemical strength in sanitized stations for wiping cloths and dishwashing machines. Quaternary ammonia test papers are one of the papers used. By immersing the strip for ten seconds in the solution it should read 200 parts per million. Iodine test strips are used when iodine is the sanitizing agent. Dipping the paper in the solution for five seconds should read 20 parts per million. (I was always highly allergic to iodine and let the operator do the testing as I observed). The most popular was the chlorine test strips as most chemically operated dishwashing machines used chlorine for sanitizing. Dipping a paper in the sanitized compartment or on a plate as it left the dishwashing machine would find 50 parts per million. When there was a deviation from these amounts corrections had to be made immediately.

Proper food storage and quality of food was always a concern for the inspector. He would enter a walk-in freezer or cooler and test the temperature first and coordinate it with the temperature gauge on the outside of the unit. The source of the food could be checked with invoices from the head chef' office. Florida, being well known for its seafood items, would cause the inspector to be aware of freshness and source of the products. The storage of items in a refrigeration unit was always noted with raw items to the lower shelves and sealed items to the top. Date marking of items and content of product listed on containers were always noted.

Tremendous investment and training by the State of Florida in its personnel to reach the status of a State Hotel and Restaurant Inspector is a continuous process. The inspector that reaches a respected status as a inspector has had years of training and attended countless number of seminars dealing with everything from fish quality to fire equipment operations and fire safety measures. Testing along the way is also completed and passed by the inspector usually on a monthly basis.

Continuing with the inspection of food service locations, we went back out to the South hallway and made a left leaving the main hotel building. We were on our way to the Poolside Kitchen. It was one of the older food service establishments and usually catered to the poolside dining room that overlooked the hotel swimming pool. It had a very large dining area and was sometimes used for the Sunday Brunch.

During this inspection I found floor tile that was in disrepair and wall surfaces that needed attention. The head of maintenance added the kitchen is schedule for a major renovation within the next month and the repairs would be addressed at that time. It was noted on the inspection report and would be re-inspected by the next routine inspection.

We then went across the driveway between the Poolside Kitchen and the next food service establishment known as the Italian Restaurant. I was told that it is only open for the dinner hour. I said I would still need to visit the kitchen and its equipment. We entered the food prep area to find a very clean appearing facility, walk-ins locked but holding temperatures accurately. The pizza ovens, grill, stoves were spotless. It was not easy to inspect a facility that was not operating but it would have to wait until I would come in the evening sometime to do a complete and thorough job.

We all left the Italian Restaurant to go back to the lobby. I excused myself to find a table and chair in the South hallway and told the assistant manager I would call her at the concierge's desk when I was ready to have her sign all the inspection forms. It was always a pleasant atmosphere to complete the day and I still had to visit a condo complex the resort hotel operated and a halfway house on their golf course

The paperwork completed and having one more opportunity to meet with this beautiful assistant manager for her signature, I bid my farewell and found my vehicle in the parking area. The remainder of the day was easy as the condo complex was in great shape and the hot dogs and hamburgers at the halfway house for the golfers only helped to improve their golfing.

CHAPTER 25

AROUND LAKE OKEECHOBEE

It happened at one time, the district I worked for, asked me to cover the route around Lake Okeechobee. I was the most likely candidate because I lived just 30 miles from the shore traveling west on highway 76 out of Stuart and pass Indiantown. So after stopping to purchase a drink of large lemonade from Ripper's Deli, onward I drove until I reached 441 at the beautiful Port Mayaca.

You will find immediately across the street from where Hwy. 76 meets Hwy 441, there is a fine looking plantation house. The two-story mansion surrounded by weeping willows and oaks trees with Spanish moss hanging from the branches, looks like it came right out of Gone With The Wind.

A middle-aged lady, who tried to restore the lodging and rebuild the kitchen area to serve meals, first owned the Inn. Unfortunately, the building was in very bad shape with a lot of termite damage, wood rot, and foundations support problems that needed special attention. Behind the main building was a servants living quarters in a separate structure. It did not appear to be in to bad a shape and the owner told me she was living there until the main Inn was completed.

I started to do an exterior investigation of the property and found it quite difficult with the overgrown vegetation. The rear of the building had a lower level that looked like it had served as a carriage house and horse barn under the Inn. I could only imagine that the horse and buggies were used to transport the earlier guests around the area and bringing them home up the gravel trail to the oval driveway. Their driver would stop at the statue of the horseman holding his ring for the reins to be received.

My attention was drawn to the concrete and brick columns that supported the building and I found that several had started to crumble. If they were to collapse the entire back of the building would fall to the ground. I had to direct the hopeful owner to see the county building department before I could do anything else for her. It would be six months later before I got another call from the Inn.

This trip found the building approved by the county and I proceeded to license the Inn for lodging. The food service had a long way to go; as she had no equipment in the two empty rooms she was going to have her kitchen. The establishment never really got off the ground before she sold the place to a private owner. I notice the building is still there and as far as I know it is just a private residence.

I went north on Hwy. 441 about thirteen miles (it always struck me funny that it was thirteen miles) and I came to the fish camp. It had to be one of the oldest on Lake Okeechobee and its atmosphere lived up to it. The camp consisted of five rustic cabins, showers, laundry, restrooms, barbeque area, and a bar serving hot dogs, hamburgers, and fish and chips. The bar also featured a pool table where you could look down from your shot and see through the floor where the catfish were swimming around waiting for crumbs to be dropped.

The cabins were always such an adventure. The beds sagged and begged for a sleeping bag to give them some support. The walls were decorated with fish done by a taxidermist many years ago. A picture on the calendar might sport a fishing boat, outboard motor, or a fishing rod and reel. There was a table big enough for a small poker game and a couple of metal tube plastic backed chairs. Sometimes the seats had holes or where covered with a cushion. The cabin was just a single room with a single light bulb hanging from the center of the ceiling.

The curtains were burlap or some very thin cotton of plain color to help keep out the sunlight. The windows were glass pane with screens but never opened due to the heavy layers of paint around the edges. From the ceiling and corners sometimes stringing to the cord holding the only light were cobwebs. I would plead with the owner to remove the cobwebs and I always got the same answer. They would say, "You want to destroy the atmosphere that makes our fisherman happy?" I supposed after fishing all day and at the bar all night, they probably didn't even notice the cobwebs.

The fire extinguishers found on the property the first time I visited were the old brass water type that had to be held upside down for the water to come out. They were located attached to a tree in front of the five units and one at the barbeque area. I informed the owners that a re-inspection would have to be made within seven days. Smoke detectors had to be placed in each unit and a hearing-impaired unit purchased.

The hearing-impaired smoke detector was a unit that would flash a 100-candelier light to wake up a deaf person. The units were quite new to the lodging industry and I was always shocked to see the very first ones invented were made of wood. They were later made of plastic and were to be hung on the doorknob when the guest was sleeping. They were also quite expensive for a five-unit fish camp. To be in compliance, I told them to visit a local fire equipment company to acquire the correct fire extinguisher, smoke detectors, and a hearing-impaired unit. The fire extinguisher had to be within fifty feet of the entrance to a unit.

Then I mentioned a rate sheet that I did not see hanging on the back of the doors for the units. "What rate did you charge for the units?" I asked.

"Whatever they can afford," was the answer.

"What was the most you ever received?" I quarried.

Twenty-five dollars is the most they had ever received and I provided them with additional rate sheets to be posted as well as having them file a copy with the district office. The rate sheets were always being removed as the thumbtack was always missing as well.

Now I had to go to the bar and found a hot dog rotisserie unit plugged into a wall socket. I asked how they cooked the hamburgers on the menu without a grill. They said they would pre-cook them at the barbeque and bring them to the bar. I opened the small counter top refrigerator and found some ground beef on the same shelf with the hot dogs. I informed them the ground beef must be kept in a separate container so the juices would not mix with the hot dogs. The bartender complied with a plastic container and lid right away. Because of the rustic nature of the establishment I recommended every food item be kept in a sealed container. Amazingly, the bartender presented me with his Food Managers card and the license was in order; their inspection was completed.

I informed them that I would be stopping back within seven days for a re-inspection of the rentals and I would stop to see them as well.

Now for a long drive around the north end of Lake Okeechobee. I would enter into Okeechobee County and pass the town of Okeechobee as I turned south on the west side of the lake onto Hwy. 78. I drove south through little villages like Buckhead Ridge, Lakeport, Moore Haven, and Clewiston, it seems like the landscape never changed. Then at South Port I had to find a motel fish camp back off the road. I had learned it was best to stop and ask so as not to waste any time. I finally found this nice clean neat looking motel with about twelve units and an owner that lived on the property. He also worked as a fishing guide on the lake and had a very Polish name that brought out the feeling that this place was going to be ship shape.

The couple that owned the motel was very up on all the regulations and freely offered the information I needed. It was a very short visit and a fine inspection that left me searching for some kind of violation. I left them a new copy of the latest regulations and they were happy that I had one in my car. They said there had not been an inspector by their place and a long time and they were beginning to worry. They were running a very fine place.

I left to head back up the east side of the lake passing through the largest town called Belle Glade. I didn't have any places other than apartment buildings. It was getting late in the afternoon by now and I wanted to get back by five in the evening. The three apartment building were quite ruff by the standards I was accustom to on the East Coast.

They were concrete with metal steps and railings extending across one side of the building. The steps were on each end and exit signs to be above each floor. The fire extinguishers were to be placed within fifty-feet of each egress from the apartments with current tags.

I found a couple of exit lights out, a railing loose on a couple of stairwells, and one or two fire extinguishers either missing, without tags current, or discharged. I could tell by some of the residence that the evenings around the area were very lively and rough with some wild antics going on. The inspections were completed and would have to be mailed to the owners, as there were no responsible people around the units to be found.

Finally, back on the road, I had completed the required inspections for the day and was homeward bound, north on Hwy. 441. Just outside Belle Glade before I got to Pahokee, I passed the Belle Glade Prison. I thought that place was pretty crowded and then I noticed flashing lights on top of a patrol car behind me. I slowed and pulled over and so did the patrol car. I young woman deputy came toward my drivers side of the car.

She said, "What's your hurry?"

I said, "I'm sorry, officer. Was I going to fast? I was done for the day and was just headed home to Stuart."

She replied, "That yellow tag on your car, tells me you don't make much more than I do and you can't afford a ticket." Just then her phone went off and she answered it. Then she said, "Your lucky day, I have to answer this robbery call. Slow it down and be careful!"

"Yes, officer I will and thank you," I breathed a sigh of relief.

As I passed through Pahokee, I thought of Mel Tillus and stuttered, "I – I – I – will never – never- never speed again." By the time I reached Port Mayaca at Hwy 76 it was four-thirty and it would take me a half an hour to reach home in Stuart. It was a full day and I looked forward to a relaxing evening with all my thoughts of the folks I had met on my tour around Lake Okeechobee.

CHAPTER 26

TEMPORARY EVENTS

The State of Florida, known for his sunny weather, is a wonderful place to hold outdoor events. The entire state is known for strawberry festivals, caladium festivals, land and sea festivals, pineapple festivals, county fairs, seafood festivals, weekend art show festivals, weekend car show festivals, and just about anything else the people of Florida can dream up to have a festival. There are entire businesses established in thc state to set up for a festival and make a substantial profit.

The business of putting on a festival is always helpful to the local economy, the vendors, and the state regulatory agencies through the licensure and inspection process. If the festival or temporary event was held in an inspector's area it was always welcomed to break the routine of everyday inspections.

A temporary food service event means any event of 30 days or less in duration where food is prepared, served, or sold to the general public. It was always brought to the district office with three days of an event, so the inspector in the area where the event was to be held could prepare his schedule. If the festival was a very large on like the Land and Sea Festival in Ft. Lauderdale or the South Florida Fair it would require anywhere from five to ten inspectors to cover the food service inspections and licensing.

I was involved for several years at the South Florida Fair and watched it grow from a number around fifty temporary food service vendors to well over one hundred vendors. All were to be inspected once they were set up on the fair grounds and ready to prepare their food items and when passing their inspection the vendors had to pay the fees required by the state. It was established that checks would not be accepted (primarily because these operators where transient and moved from festival to festival and many from out of state), but money orders or cash was the normal means of pay.

This would worry most of the inspectors because they would have to carry several amounts of money around a temporary event and they had to be very careful. I don't want to say that the vendors were not to be trusted but the people roaming around a festival before it opens was always a concern. Luckily, in my tenure there was never an incident. But, at one time in the state there was a case where inspectors had lost the fees collected and the state began to look for other ways of collecting these license fees.

It is almost beyond ones imagination to the extent vendors will go to promote their products over the competing vendors at a temporary event. Each will have its signs with the name of their food, streamers, balloons, music, and anything else that will entice the customer to buy their product over another located just within steps away. The locations can be rigs like large trailers, small pop-up tents covering tables, ice cream trucks, or my favorite was the two-story cotton candy trailer. Some became very elaborate with reach-in freezers, reach-in refrigerators, deep fat fryers, and steam tables, ready to sell all they had brought to the event.

Some of the temporary food service establishments had refrigerated trucks brought in to store their products, so as not to run out of stock. These also had to be inspected by the inspectors. Those temporary food service units that had local licensed restaurants could operate under that same license. Still, all food service personnel had to have a food safety certificate card showing their completion of the course. This was to ensure the food handlers understood the safety requirements necessary to serve the public.

Many of the same inspection requirements for permanent restaurants also applied to temporary food service establishments. Temperature controls had to be met, fire protection must be in place, utensils and equipment had to be in good condition with adequate storage, floor surfaces had to be sealed, three compartment sink facilities provided for washing and sanitizing everything, and most important hand washing sinks provided with soap, sanitized water, and towels.

The early days of the South Florida Fair found a very necessary inspection of drainage from waste water and storage containers had to be used by everyone. The containers had to be sealed and kept out of the way from the public. The containers had to be kept empty and not cause a public health threat by overflowing. Ground water was always a concern as hoses were tightly fit and all drips attended to immediately. Later as the fair grew in size, so did the facilities for sewage. Drainage was installed underground a central dumping stations were built.

The biggest problem was the timely arrival of the temporary event food service units, setting them up, and being prepared for the inspection prior to the opening of the first day of the event. Most of the vendors would travel from one event to another and new the procedure required by the state. These were the professionals, but then there were the independent folks that wanted to be a part of event and came at the last minute or even a day later. This was finally addressed, and they were found to be operating illegally and subject to fines. It created a problem for inspectors that did not want to work late into the evenings or return to the event for licensing again. There was always an event coordinator that was in charge of an event and worked with the state to see that this problem was kept under control.

With each event there were always memories of certain incidents or relationships with the event or festival. The larger ones would almost become a blur because the same units came year after year. They would greet the inspector as a long lost friend and the inspector would try and remember their face or name from all those he had met throughout the year. Some were always well prepared and took their jobs very professionally. They were the ones that were set up on time, had their paperwork in order and never gave us a bad time with their fees. Their units were well organized, clean, and prepared to have a great time and most of all make a lot of money.

Then there were those we were on the lookout for that always gave us trouble. They would either show up at the very last minute, or their training documents were outdate, fire equipment outdated, or they pretended they didn't know there was a fee for operating. These kinds of problems were not very prevalent but still caused some grief.

Since the subtitle for this book is the Memoirs I suppose it would be expected to hear about some of these establishments at the temporary events. The first being the good was easy to enjoy. The best was an organization built on providing festivals with a full assortment of foods, facilities, and personnel trained to make their festival a big success. A husband and wife team operated this business and they were easy to work with. They would provide the inspector with a cart and chauffer to get to all their locations. The facilities were usually joined by a long tent and separated by walls or equipment serving different foods. The front of the tents and serving tables were separated from the lines of people by white picket fences.

The inspection and licensing went very fast because they were so organized in the state's regulations on temporary events. They also were set up to have a money order or cash for the entire amount of their different establishments. They were highly respected by the inspectors and were found to do business throughout the state at different festivals.

Another one of the good temporary event operators was a growing company in my own back yard of Martin County. When I say they were a growing company I mean to say they started out under a tent at the local Flea Market and grew into an international event business. The company started to but on birthday parties and grew to putting up bleachers at the Indianapolis 500 races, parties in California, and extravagant weddings with white tablecloths, tents, and silver service buffets. The last event I remember them catering was the opening of Donald Trumps Millionaire Club at Mar-a-Logo in Palm Beach, Florida. Shortly afterwards some investors entered his business and made him an offer he could not refuse and he is retired now as a wealthy multi-millionaire. Hard work and doing things first class, the right way, the first time was his key to success.

I'll never forget the day he called me and asked what he had to do to get a hot dog cart licensed to operate. I asked him why he would want to do such a thing. His' response was that he had gotten board and wanted something to do. Last I heard he was off on a trip to Europe and bought another house in Mississippi.

The bad would have to be one of the festivals that were rained on from the first day through out till the end of the festival. Yes, this does happen in Florida during our rainy season but sometimes when it is not the rainy season also. The rain can come down in buckets and it makes everything a mess. The wind can blow and tents go flying, the water floods the food preparation area, or vehicles get stuck in mud, and everyone wants to just give up and go home.

This happened on one occasion at a festival called the Sun Fest in West Palm Beach.

Everyone showed up with all the expectations of having a great festival. Everyone except Mother Nature who decided to forget all the weatherman's predictions of a dry weekend and brought a deluge of rain. This happened to the best operator I know for temporary events and we all had to do our best to complete our task of inspecting each food service operation and licensing them. That year the Sun Fest was a bust and we all felt it with the loss of sales to the economy and the lack of people attending the festival.

The event that had a very serious problem before I was an inspector in the area experienced what we all hate to hear about. It seems a worn power cord running from food vendors to a power supply was left on the ground and a rainstorm caught everyone off guard. A person was walking by the wet ground and the electrical cord sent a shock through the person's body that killed him. The event was immediately closed and the future temporary events were subject to much closer inspection by health inspectors and fire marshal's.

It happened at the very same event many years later when my fellow inspector and I were covering this event that we had a very ugly encounter with a couple of Haitian ladies. They had arrived very late for the temporary event and started to unload their van. A couple of the vendors that were already inspected and license gave us the heads up.

When we rounded the corner and found pots turned upside down and crates of vegetables, boxes of lettuce and cabbage, and a bushel of apples on the ground, we immediately looked for the owners. Pretty soon, here came a couple of heavy weight ladies, their hair bound up in handkerchiefs, their long dressed swaying as the strode towards their spot in their thronged sandals.

We introduced ourselves and asked what they were going to present at the festival. They replied they have a restaurant north of here and they were going to prepare their native salads to serve to the customers. We asked the name of the restaurant and neither one of us had ever heard of it. They said they had been licensed and they would be operating under the same license so they would not have to purchase a temporary event license.

This led us to believe the ladies had some knowledge of the food industry requirements in the State of Florida. We asked if they had a copy of the license and they said it was back in the van they had driven in to the festival. Now, we were a little more hopeful that this was going to be a nice situation and the ladies knew what they were attempting to do.

One of the ladies immediately got out a head of cabbage and started to cut it up on the surface of the pot that was turned upside down. The knife was a very large butcher knife and was cutting through that cabbage head with ease as she chopped a few more and threw them aside into another pot. She did not have any water present, never washed her hands, or wiped anything off except the sweat that was starting to run down her face from her forehead.

The first lady returned with a restaurant license. My partner looked it over and asked her if she realized the license had expired last year and was not current. She said there must have been a mistake and it was just a clerical error. My partner called our district office and verified that the license had been paid by a bad check and they had never renewed the original license. Many attempts had been made by the department to collect the amount as well as the penalty fees but the owners of the business could never be located.

We explained their dilemma and told them we could collect the money at this time if they were ready to pay. No, no they were just here to participate in the temporary event.

While we were talking to our district office the two ladies continued to chop up lettuce, snap vegetables, and chop carrots, and threw everything into a pot. Finally, we asked to please stop until we straighten out this problem with their license. They said they could not for two reasons; first they did not own the restaurant and second they only worked for the restaurant.

They had not brought any water with them, any soap or hand towels, and only rags to wipe their hands. We tried to explain all the necessary equipment, food handlers training certification, and sanitary items like a three compartment sink and hand sink that had to be available for use. They said they were going to prepare their food the way they had always done in the islands and that people loved their food.

When we told them they could not be at the festival as a food vendor they became very agitated and started to speak in Haitian very load and rapidly. They were not stopping their preparations of the unwashed vegetables, cabbage, or utensils. I asked what they planned on doing with the pot full of cabbage, vegetables, and other things. They said had a burner with propane gas to set on the ground and they would boil everything and serve it as a soup. They would go buy some water from the store or get it from a hose on the ground somewhere.

After several attempts to get the ladies to understand that they could not participate in the temporary event we decided to get the director of the event to support our position. It took awhile to locate him and all the while the ladies continued to prepare their brew and wipe their sweating brows and arms from the 90-degree weather we were all enjoying.

Finally, the director of the temporary event showed up and the ladies were asked to leave the area. Disgruntled, angry, and completely unhappy, the ladies and their pots loaded up their van and drove away. The information was recorded and was later used by the department as the ladies kept trying to participate in other temporary events throughout our district. The food service and preparation might have been loved in Haiti and the islands but not loved by the inspectors or temporary event people.

One year when I was assigned to work the South Florida Fair in West Palm Beach, we decided to try something a little different in the licensing process. We had a team of about six inspectors and sent four out on the grounds to inspect each vendor leaving the operator with a copy of a satisfactory inspection report. They were told to go to the main fair building to see two inspectors, showing the inspection report, pay their license fee, and be issued a temporary event license to be posted inside their food service facility.

This worked so well, as the money was not carried all around the grounds, they facility for writing licenses was much more satisfactory, and let the operators be involved in the process with a little more responsibility on their part. It process was so successful that I decide to use the same tactic at the Martin County Fair to be held immediately following the South Florida Fair.

The events were smaller back then and now I understand the process is done with several golf carts and a crew of inspectors that accomplish the same process with just as much speed and efficiency. We were always prepared to handout signs for temperature controls, hand washing, and sanitary process for food contact surfaces. The vendors were always so appreciative of receiving something from the state even when it was just a sign or reminder of how things were to be done to assure a safe temporary event.

Temporary events were so popular for the people operating foodservice units that a good fair or event would generate around five hundred to eight hundred dollars per day. The only curse was the possibility of a rainy and the event became a loss but then there was always a sunny tomorrow and another temporary event.

CHAPTER 27

THE E. R. BRADLEY RESTAURANT

The twenty-four years inspecting food service facilities in South Florida it became apparent to me that I had enjoyed the growth of the Bradley Restaurant. It seems the Bradley name came to my attention for the first time while reading a Brown Wrapper in the Sunday edition of The Palm Beach Post. I was very interested in all the history of the Palm Beaches as related in the Brown Wrappers. They were published by a dear friend of mine named Judge James R. Knott.

I would like to share a bit of history with you about Edward R. Bradley for whom the present restaurant was named after. You see the Bradley Restaurant started in Palm Beach and later moved to West Palm Beach. It is located at the end of Clematis and overlooks the Inter Coastal Waterway. But originally it was known at the Bradley's Beach Club.

1 BRADLEY'S BEACH CLUB
April 3, 1983

The Beach Club, known simply as Bradley's, was for years the most celebrated, the most glamorous and exclusive gambling casino in the United States. A "must" for the rich and famous who came to Palm Beach, its stakes were high, its rules were strict, and scandal never touched its name. Residents of Florida could not qualify for membership or enter the gambling rooms.

Edward R. Bradley, owner-founder of the Beach Club, born 1859, was the son of Irish immigrants. He left his native Pennsylvania to become a professional gambler in the Far West during his twenties, and later lived in Chicago. With his brother John Bradley he operated the Bacchus Club in St. Augustine in the 1890's. He came to Palm Beach and established the Beach Club in 1898. During the rest of his long life he was to become a commanding and greatly respected figure in that sophisticated community. Col. Bradley was also widely known in the racing world. With his renowned Idle Hour Farm at Lexington, Kentucky, he was the first four-time winner of the Kentucky Derby. The colors of his silks, green and white, were carried over for the decorative scheme of the Beach Club.

According to the *New York World*, "The real reason for the popularity of Palm Beach is not its climate or its hotels; it is Bradley's." A 1930 article in *Collier's Weekly* termed it "the sportiest and classiest gambling house in the world." It operated as a private club every season for 48 years until shortly before his death in 1947, the longest unlawful gambling operation in the history of the United States.

Reform waves, investigations, taxcs and other outside influences never affected it. With its own platoon of Pinkerton men, substantial control of local publicity media, political contributions, generous donations to charities and churches of all denominations, Bradley's was virtually a law unto itself.

Due largely to the unique personality of Bradley himself, his Beach Club generated much of the color and drama associated with the heyday of Palm Beach.

The Beach Club was located on the site of the present Bradley Park near the Lake Trail, just north of the old railroad bridge (replaced by the present Flagler, or north, bridge). There, trains *backed* across the lake to deliver passengers to the Royal Poinciana and Breakers hotels.

Bradley's was a sprawling white frame structure, commodious and comfortable in appearance, surrounded by lawns and palm trees. It looked innocent enough, but it was indeed a gambler's paradise where fortunes could and did change hands with a spin of the wheel.

In the old days, as trains from the north arrived at the Palm Beach station via the railroad bridge which used to span Lake Worth, the enormous bulk of the Royal Poinciana Hotel stretched out on one side of the train. On the other side, directly opposite the station, was Bradley's, Palm Beach's most celebrated "charitable" institution – charitable because it assisted people who had more money than they knew what to do with to get rid of some of it in a quiet, socially acceptable way.

Palm Beachers of earlier days loved to gamble. Gurnee Munn Jr. told this writer about being in a private railroad car in Palm Beach during the '20s and seeing a group of men around a table containing a pile of money and checks. His father gestured toward the table and told him that it held more than a million dollars. Alva Johnston, the writer, told of Josh Cosden taking a pot of $875,000 in a poker gam3e with Harry Payne Whitney, J. L. Replogie and others. In those days, some of the heavy betters used to throw as much as 10,000 shares of blue chip stock in the pot.

During wartime, when gasoline was rationed, ladies in evening finery and gentlemen in dinner jackets were seen peddling bicycles with as much dignity as they could muster on their way to Bradley's. And they came on buses from Boca Raton and Delray Beach when rationed gas for automobiles was hard to obtain. It is not surprising that when Bradley's closed with the colonel's death, the late Joseph P. Kennedy said, "Palm Beach has lost its zipperoo."

The *New York Journal-American* carried an article by columnist Bill Corum on August 16, 1946, the day after Bradley's death, stating that "Bradley was as honest as the day is long," and that when he died "some of the greatest stories that one of the best known and highest stake gamblers the world has ever known died with him. As did an era, and one of the last links of an America that used to be." The article continued:

"There won't be any more Ed Bradleys. In Palm Beach and on various race courses of the nation from Saratoga and Churchill Downs to Hialeah, or anywhere else. And one thing that guarantees the truth of that sweeping statement is the income tax.

"Nobody could possibly play in these days for the sort of stakes that almost surely made that modest looking casino in Palm Beach the home of the highest rolling gambling the world has ever seen.

"No songs were ever written about it, such as 'He broke the bank at Monte Carlo.' It never had the worldwide fame of that Azure Coast and perhaps two or three other famous temples of chance. But when they were rolling 'em big in the lush money and moon days and nights at Palm Beach, more was won and lost on one whirl of the little ball or the turn of a card than ever in the history of the world had been won or lost before."

Bradley gave complete protection to the socialites whose pursuit of pleasure was instrumental in supporting his operation. As stated in *The New York Times*, "The Club at Palm Beach survived all reform waves, and had the respect and support of the society leaders and industrial giants who made Palm Beach their winter home."

It was not unusual to see an oil or steel magnate place five hundred dollars or more in chips on the board at each turn of the wheel, and drop fifteen or twenty thousand dollars in a few minutes. John Studebaker, the auto maker, and "Bet-a-million" Gates were among those who thought nothing of dropping $200,000 in an evening of roulette.

During the period of the Beach Club's operation, there was little the wealthy had to worry about except the possibility that idle gossip could be fanned into scandal by the press. There was never any scandal at all about Bradley's. In fact, there were few reports of any kind. The colonel saw to that with his choice of croupiers, cashiers, dealers, and the rules he laid down for their lives and behavior during the season.

They were not permitted to bring their wives to Florida with them during the working season. Bradley knew that even the close-mouthed clan of croupiers are human too, and preferred not to take the chance of tidbits regarding the details of his operations and stories about his guests being communicated by his employees to their families.

Servants as well as gambling room employees lived and remained on the premises throughout the season. Bradley admitted frankly that he had never kept books on the place, because such books might have been incriminating under Florida law. He never even kept a payroll, apparently because the salaries of employees, ranging as high as $100 a day (reduced to $50 in the Depression), were held back until the end of the season except for an allowance for incidentals.

Bradley and his wife, Agnes, were a devoted couple, although she did not spend much time in Florida. Mrs. Bradley died in 1925 while on a world cruise with a party of friends.

She was an enthusiastic but haphazard bettor. Once she conceived a system of betting on all horses in each race except the favorite. Bradley told Mose Cossman, his personal betting commissioner, to handle the bets and then privately instructed him to hold them back. It worked very well until Mrs. Bradley hit a 1,000 to 1 shot and Bradley had to pay her $18,855 from his own pocket. He never told her what he had done.

Bradley was a man who set much store on deep loyalty. His employees, whether on his breeding farm, at his gambling establishment or in his business pursuits, invariably stayed with him for years. Many died in harness, so to speak. None of his dealers was ever known to drop so much as a hint of what went on inside the club, or who won or lost how much, or what gentleman turned up with whose wife.

People reminiscing about old times recall the story about the wife who used to extract uncashed chips from her husband's clothes whenever he played at Bradley's, and cashed them in for twenty-five thousand dollars without her husband knowing that he had lost anything.

Although Bradley was known for his discernment, his judgment of people was not quite infallible. An illustration of this is given by Cleveland Armory in his book *The Last Resorts*. He tells the well known story of the young lady who came into Bradley's private office at the club one night, tears in her eyes, and told him that she and her husband were on their honeymoon in Palm Beach, and that her husband had just lost their entire savings of $5,000.

Bradley looked at her closely, then reached in his drawer and took out five $1,000 bills. "I'll give you these," he said, "on condition you promise me that neither you nor your husband will ever enter this club again." Still tearful, the girl agreed.

The next night the colonel, touring his tables, was brought up short; there was the young man the girl had described as her husband, gambling away as if nothing had happened. Bradley immediately sent for the man.

"You were told never to come here again," he stormed. "you cannot afford that kind of money. Your wife agreed."

The young man smilled. "Colonel Bradley," he said, "I am not married." It turned out that he was a son of Harvey Firestone.

Up to the time of his death, Bradley was asked by those who had heard the story what he did about it.

"I didn't do a thing," the colonel would say. "Any girl who can get the best of a tough old goat like me is welcome to $5,000."

In the evenings the smart thing to do was to go over to the Beach Club. By half past nine o'clock every night Bradley's was so crowded, according to an observer, that one "almost had to fight his way from table to table."

Bradley's was different from gambling houses in other American resorts, which were often havens for crooks. Bradley's was run exclusively for the wealthy northern patrons of Palm Beach. Almost everybody who went to Bradley's could afford to lose and lose heavily, and a list of the people who played there every night would include many of America's leading social and financial names. The fact that it was outside the law was quite irrelevant.

The big octagonal gambling salon at the end of a long green hall leading from the dining room (which was serviced by a crew of fifty) contained six roulette tables and two tables for French hazard, a game similar to chuck-o-luck. For the hazard tables, Bradley employed old-time professional dealers who he had known in the west during his youth.

A back room contained one hazard table and seven roulette tables. In the beginning men only were admitted to this room – usually those whose wives objected to their gambling for high stakes. The prohibition against women in the back room was lifted when it became apparent that many ladies were fond of high stakes themselves.

Many of Bradley's patrons were accustomed to playing chemin de fer (a game similar to baccarat) in Europe, and asked Bradley to install a table for that purpose. To accommodate them, he built a second floor room in 1923, where three chemin de fer tables were set in operation. French dealers were brought over from Europe to deal the game. The stakes were at first unlimited, but the patrons' occasional wild over-indulgence which led them to risk over $100,000 on a single "bank" caused the establishment of a $5,000 limit on each play for their own protection.

Individual winnings at the Beach Club were paid off only in new bills. Bradley always kept up to $1,000,000 in new bills as spare cash in his office safe.

Around the walls, high above the heads of the players in the octagonal room, there was a white trellis, behind which there were guards armed with machine guns. Bradley's employed 28 guards, each assigned by written instructions to a specific post in the event of an emergency, and Bradley himself said that if any gangsters or robbers ever go in, "they would have to fight their way out." In the entire history of the club there was never a holdup.

Members of the club were invited to sign a card placing a self-imposed limit on themselves for a single evening which could not be changed during the heat of a game. If a guest, when unobserved, lost more than his stated limit, the club assumed responsibility for the difference because of its failure to keep check on his activities.

Bradley demanded proper decorum on the part of his guests, and carefully handpicked his membership. A new member had to be introduced by an old member, who thereby accepted responsibility for his social and moral (but not financial) character. As a concession to reformists and the morals of the state, residents of Florida engaged in business in the state were not admitted to the club according to the by-laws, and any resident of the state could be effectively excluded from membership in the club and entrance to the gambling rooms. Only members or guests of members were admitted even to the dining room. No man who appeared to be under the influence of liquor was permitted to enter the club. And in the evening, no man was allowed in the club without formal attire. Under the by-laws male guests had to be 25 years of age and appear to be that age to gain entrance to the club.

Ohan Berberyan, the well-known New York rare rug dealer, told a story about the membership rules being relaxed in a special case:

"Once I had a prominent Palm Beach physician as a dinner guest at the Beach Club.

After dinner, Col. Bradley asked me not to bring the doctor in again, as he was opposed to permitting local residents to be seen at the gambling club. Some weeks after this incident, when a dinner guest at the Beach Club was choking on a piece of steak that had lodged in his windpipe, an emergency call for my doctor friend, an outstanding eye, ear, nose and throat specialist, perhaps saved the life of the man, who happened to be John Hylan, the Mayor of New York. Before the doctor left the club, the colonel personally made out a membership card for him. This made the doctor the only Palm Beach local member of the gambling club."

Political interference was rare, largely because the morals and pocketbooks of Florida citizens could not truthfully be said to be adversely affected by the club and because of Bradley's towering reputation for person integrity and generosity in charitable fields. Nevertheless, Bradley was prepared to meet unexpected situations.

At one time Florida's Governor Park Trammell was widely criticized from the pulpit wand in the press for allowing Bradley's gambling to operate. He finally dispatched a trusted personal representative to make a confidential investigation, in 1915.

The Governor's agent came by train unannounced and without fanfare. His arrival at the station in West Palm Beach happened to be observed by Joe Earman, a local newspaper publisher who knew him and was also well acquainted with Col. Bradley. The agent, secure in the knowledge that it was too late for Bradley to receive timely warning of his visit, confided the purpose of his trip to Joe Earman. Earman excused himself just long enough to warn Bradley by phone, and then offered to take the visitor to the casino. Immediately afterward, the two left for Bradley's in order to catch the place by surprise.

And what a surprise! The gaming tables had been whisked out, the orchestra had been moved from the hall near the dinning area to the main gambling room, and everyone was happily dancing away. In due course, the Governor received his representative's report and solemnly announced to the people of Florida that his investigation showed that the rumors about gambling going on at Bradley's were absolutely untrue.

To illustrate the sanctity in which he held his reputation Bradley, in turning his property over to the Town of Palm Beach under the terms of his will, specified that the building should be demolished and the land used as a park. He did this as a precaution to guard his reputation, stating to a trusted employee and friend that unless the building were destroyed it might be used for gambling by unscrupulous operator, and under his name, in which event his own good reputation would suffer.

The impressive ornamental lamps on the pylons at the east entrance to Palm Beach's Flagler Bridge were given by Bradley as a decorative appurtenance to the Palm Beach scene. He obtained them from the London residence of the Duke of Devonshire when it was razed to make way for The Dorchester Hotel in Mayfair.

Col. Bradley's Idle Hour Farm at Lexington was a notable racing stable. But his gambling, rather than his racing stable, made him conspicuously wealthy. Aristocratic in appearance and demeanor, he was a man of strict honely, impeccable taste, suavity and discretion. With all his worldly interests, he was a devout Catholic. He gave three-quarters ($600,000) of the cost of St. Edward's Church in Palm Beach, and often donated anonymously to churches of other denominations. He did not regard gambling as necessarily evil or harmful for those who could afford to lose, but counseled against it for those who could not afford to lose.

The colonel, who had an unusual facility in dealing with figures – and odds, was scrupulously careful about his income tax returns. He prepared a separate return for his Beach Club operations, reporting income based upon a percent of the gross amount of the betting. When the Internal Revenue department expressed some doubt about the correctness of his figures, two agents were sent at his invitation to Palm Beach, where they stayed in a hotel at Bradley's expense for two weeks in order to observe the operations of his club at first hand. At the end of that period they expressed the conclusion that the colonel's figures were weighed to the advantage of the government, rather than the taxpayer.

He was frank about his profession. Years ago, when the late Huey Long sought to embarrass him before a senate investigating committee, the even-tempered colonel was asked his business.

Bradley replied: "I am a breeder of thoroughbred race horses, a speculator and a gambler."

"What do you bet on?"

"Anything," said E.R.

Senator Long then asked, "Is it not a fact that you own the biggest gambling house in America, located in Palm Beach?" At this, Senator Pat Harrison, chairman of the committee, ruled that Bradley did not have to answer the question, and that Senator Long's inquiry would be confined to matters regarding Louisiana. Senator Long then asked Bradley if he did not have gambling interests in that state.

"My partner, John P. Sullivan, and I own the Louisiana Jockey Club," Bradley replied. "And I might say that I contributed $5,000 to your campaign fund, through Sullivan," he added.

"That's a d—lie!" Huey blustered.

"Why, Senator," Bradley went on, blandly, "don't you remember thanking me for that contribution, in the lobby of the Roosevelt Hotel?" The senator, remembering, dismissed the witness.

And indeed he would bet on anything. When a certain patron, then 83, exuberantly announced to Bradley that he was marrying a very young woman, the colonel's gambling sense became alerted. He offered his friend a bet and put $10,000 in bills on his desk. "I'll bet you this $10,000 that you won't live a year after you marry her," he said. The bridegroom agreed to the bet, put up $10,000 and the money was deposited in Bradley's safe. The groom's death was announced a few weeks later, in England, during along honeymoon tour with his bride.

There are many stories of Bradley's dealing with his patrons, some doubtless exaggerated, but unquestionably all with some basis in fact. When you hear of Bradley tearing up half of the I.O.Us of a woman who had overreached herself to the tune of $25,000, because he knew her husband would stand for her losing $12,500 in an evening, but no more, one suspects a considerable basis of fact. Bradley knew just how far each of his customers was able to go, and they were not allowed credit beyond that amount (only three women in Palm Beach were allowed unlimited credit).

A motion picture magnate reportedly lost $300,000 one night and signed I.O.U.s for the amount, as was customary. Later, when asked for payment at the club, the man claimed fraud. Bradley then and there asked for his membership card, tore it up and counted it as "water over the dam." This story has been authenticated, though the exact amount involved cannot be verified. In the rare case of a patron expressing the thought that his loses might be due to something besides bad luck, it was Bradley's established policy to forget the debt and ask that the membership card be surrendered in his presence.

There is also the authenticated story of the lady who collapsed and died with a heart attack while being wheeled back to the Royal Poinciana from Bradley's one night. She had lost $100,000.

If you lost heavily one evening, the colonel invariably offered you at the door one throw of a coin – double or nothing. He would throw the coin, and the patron would call it. Bradley had an interesting theory about this policy. A friend now residing in the Palm Beach area once asked him whether the custom was a profitable one. He replied that he had kept records over a period of 40 years which showed that he was the winner three times out of five on these occasions, and ventured an explanation which conformed to one of his favorite theories regarding the gambling business – the existence of losing and winning streaks.

"It's like this," said the colonel. "If a man finds himself a big winner at the end of an evening, he's satisfied, and not at all inclined to risk his 'hard-earned' winnings on one toss. On the other hand, a man who has lost heavily is likely to risk a bet on double or nothing. When he has such a losing streak, my figures show that he will lose three times out of five. My own rule is to press good luck (increase the size of bets during a winning streak), but take it easy on a bad streak."

Bradley illustrated this practice by citing his experience during a period at Latonia race track where he bet on each of the six races run each day, six days each week for two weeks, and had 72 straight losing bets before his luck changed. When it became obvious to him that he was going to lose consistently until the end of the losing streak was reached, he commenced betting nominal sums (less than $50) rather than increasing his bets to get even. His only purpose in continuing to bet was to "break the streak."

He was sometimes very lucky. Ohan Berberyan said in a letter to this writer that "When the colonel invited me to join him at supper once, I ordered what he ordered. He demurred. Although it was a bit too rich for his blood, as he was then on a restricted diet, he wanted me to order caviar and champagne. When I wanted to know the occasion for the celebration, he told me that he had sold his interest in Hialeah Park to Joe Kennedy the day before, and a few hours later President Roosevelt issued a war order closing all tracks, to save gasoline. I think he was the largest individual shareholder at that time, Joseph Widener having the other shares, so the Colonel was celebrating."

The colonel did not like to see men gamble who could not afford to lose and usually took advantage of an opportunity to discourage them from gambling. A former member of his staff recalls his giving that advice to a would-be gambler whom he did not wish to go "overboard." Bradley observed that "hard money can't win," i.e., that where a man is losing and cannot afford it, his mind does not function properly and he starts playing desperately, with disastrous results.

Until he was faced with an unusual occurrence Bradley allowed the Beach Club to operate around the clock. One night a wealthy gambler found himself in debt to the roulette wheel to the tune of $135,000. He kept playing with determination, so that near eight o'clock the following morning the wheel owed him close to the amount he had owed the wheel a few hours earlier. Bradley, suspecting his own stature might be diminished by players who didn't know when to quit, set new hours for operating between 1:00 p.m. and 4:00 a.m.

Whether the famous Dr. Rhine and his ESP (extrasensory perception) department at Duke University would substantiate the colonel's theories about winning and losing streaks is not known. However, the fact remains that the colonel was undeniably a very successful gambler and died a wealthy man. 1.

So, when I got a call from a Mr. Frank Coniglio in regards to opening a Bradley's Hotel and Restaurant, I was extremely excited. To bring back the history of a Bradley's to Palm Beach, but without the gambling was quite a leap. I first was introduced to this project during a meeting with Mr. Coniglio. He was full of enthusiasm and wanted every minute of my time to see what he was up against with the current rules and regulations from the state of Florida.

At the time we were allowed several minutes of information stop if we had completed all of our required inspections for the day. I looked over the blueprints that had been prepared and found that the establishment was to be located across the street from the original Bradley's Beach Club. It was the location of a hotel that the original club had constructed for its special guests.

The new E. R. Bradley's as it was to be named consisted of apartments on a first floor and second floor with the use of an elevator and secondary staircase that opened to a central courtyard. East of the courtyard was an entrance into a dining area and bar. It was very small and could accommodate approximately fifty people. Later there would be a small outside dining area just to the north.

The many visits for information and assistance in how he wanted the rental units, bar equipment and kitchen equipment furnished to meet the regulations and pass his opening inspections. The apartments were ready

1 The Best of the Brown Wrappers I, **PALM BEACH REVISTED,** Historical Vignettes of Palm Beach County, by James R. Knott.

first. The furnishings were very nice, the electric smoke detectors, exit signs, double locks, and fire alarms as well as a licensed elevator and I was able to issue the State of Florida Public Lodging license. I don't believe the first residence was prepared for the finishing construction noise that was necessary to complete the food service area. Floor drains were jack hammered in place, equipment being delivered at all hours of the day and night but the opening day was in sight. It would be after several return trips to the E. R. Bradley's Restaurant before the final inspection and the State of Florida Public Foodservice license was issued.

Frank Coniglio was a great promoter and the bar would be packed during happy hours, sporting events, and private parties. I remember the inspections were always made more difficult during an event and the bar area was so crowded and the noise was always very much like the decorum I could imagine at the Bradley's Beach Club. The lodgings were always a pleasure to inspect because the inspection would be mostly exterior as the units were full of guests.

I was called out of the area to work out of Orlando for a while and I lost the town of Palm Beach to another inspector. During my hyenas E. R. Bradley's made a historical move. A fantastic location across the Inter coastal waterway became available and Frank Coniglio decided to move the restaurant. True to the original founder, Frank was a gambler and it was a risky move but a sure fire success. The new E. R. Bradley's is now located at the 104 Clematis Street, West Palm Beach.

My many years following the relocation I had only inspected the new E. R. Bradley's one time. I found the operation of the staff and facility to be top notch and the colonel would have been proud. Frank Coniglio is a man of great dedication and honesty as his establishment is always at the forefront of the latest requirements of the state of Florida in training his staff on food safety and meeting all the laws covering food service. He is always there to assist in any way he can to assure that the state is satisfied and he is always volunteering to help the inspection of the Sun Festival, which is held almost in his front yard.

CHAPTER 28

MEMORABLE PLACES

Over the years an inspector has the pleasure of inspecting so many different places. Some of them stick in your mind because of certain things that might have happened during the inspection or you met a particular person of interest or you can remember helping a property owner or establishment owner that was so grateful for your help.

It was while being called to a new golf course in the Hobe Sound area that I was surprised to run into a professional golfer who I did not meet in person but I did see him walking off the putting green with his putter held over his shoulders. I had just inspected his halfway house that served hot dogs and cold sandwiches. The professional golfer I speak of used to fly a helicopter back and forth from his home on Jupiter Island. I'm sure he did not hear me but I called to him to say he was now legal as his hot dog stand was selling hot dogs for over a month. I won't mention his name but will say he was from Australia and that should nail his name down. He also had the largest Great White Shark hanging in the member's bar where they said women were not allowed.

Then I was inspecting another bar in Lake Park one day and was surprised to find the bar was owned by a famous pool player that had appeared in the movie The Hustler. He was very polite and interested in how I went about my duties as a health inspector. I was interested in his profession because I told him I worked my way through college managing a pool hall on campus. He was impressed and was even more impressed when I showed him that his bartenders were not using the three compartment sink properly and was failing to clean out the beer coolers adequately. We talked again on the re-inspection and he was not behind the eight ball anymore.

I had the pleasure of meeting a hall of fame pitcher that owned a bar in Jupiter. He was very friendly and was not disturbed when I told him I had never seen him pitch but had seen his trading card before. I tried to help him out with a problem he was having with Alcohol and Tobacco. It almost got me into a lot of trouble because they thought I was interfering with another state departments business.

It seems he had a certain type of alcohol license that was permitted under the stipulation that food would always be available to his customers as long as the bar was open. The cook would go home at 10 o'clock p.m. and the evening bar tender was to get the food from the kitchen when it was ordered after that hour. It seems the bartender felt he had enough to do in serving drinks and would refuse to accept food orders. It happened the first time to an undercover A&T official and the owner was given a warning. The second time it happened, the same bartender again refused to serve food and the licensee was to pay a very steep fine to the A&T Board.

When I tried to speak for the owner and give the A&T department my opinion of his establishment and their record with our department, I was told to mind my business and not to cross department areas ever again. Eventually, the owner had to put the license in his daughters name to protect the license for the business.

The fact that he was in baseballs hall-of-fame did nothing for his two strikes and your out.

When I was working out of the Orlando office for the state of Florida, I was attending an all day meeting at the district office in Orlando. My wife came along and we were staying at a hotel right next door to the office. The meeting got over and I went back to the hotel expecting to see my wife waiting for me. Instead, I found a note in our room saying she had gone to Universal Studios with a few of the other wives. She would return in the evening.

So, I made myself comfortable in the lobby and enjoyed the music being played on a grand piano. It was very interesting watching people come and go through the hotel lobby. All of a sudden I saw this very large man that I recognized as a professional basketball player that played for the Orlando Magic. When he came through the main door of the hotel he had to stoop over to get under the top of the door.

Waiting for my wife's arrival I decided I would surprise her and requested our favorite song to be played by the pianist. I would give him the (excuse the pun) heads up, when she arrived. She finally arrived to the tune of Unforgettable.

Not as popular but just as important in my career as a state health inspector, I will never forget the oriental couple that had just received their restaurant license and the very next day I stood with them outside of that same restaurant and watched it burn to the ground. They were in total shock. They were so young and hadn't gotten around to signing their insurance policy on the business. It was their very first venture.

Years later, again I licensed their new restaurant in Jupiter and they went on to a very successful enterprise. It was so heartwarming to see this young couple stick to it and enjoy the success of a good restaurant. They eventually married and had a beautiful baby. I retired and hated to end the relationship we had because we never forgot that fire at their first restaurant.

Then there was a very swanky private club in Jupiter that had a hotel and two kitchens as well as a halfway house on their golf course. They used to make me so mad because they would make me wait in the lobby and it would take me to long to get to the food service before I could start the inspections. I would really take my time in return and make sure I never missed the slightest violation just to pay them back. They always set a tone of better than anyone else and kind of looked down on everything you would tell them.

I never got to meet the famous Canadian singer resident that lived in their posh club. She had the biggest house, but never let her fame and fortune stand in her way of being just like any other common person. She would go up to Albertson grocery shopping or her husband would go to a Chinese takeout and leave a generous tip. They never put on airs and would go out of their way to make others feel comfortable around them.

The club members got upset with them because they acted that way and the members did not like that they treated others like they wanted to be treated. Eventually, the resident left their uppity club and moved to another in Jupiter that was developed by a famous golfer that resides in Florida.

Back in Martin County I will always have a fond memory of a place called The Dolphin Bar and Shrimp House. It fronts the Indian River and can be found just north of Sewalls Point on the Indian River Drive.

The restaurant and resort originally was called The Outrigger. The Outrigger was designed as a Polynesian restaurant and included three duplex guest quarters. The property provided a marina for boats and eventually the owner's 208-foot yacht.

The owners name was Francis Langford, a successful radio, recording, and film and T.V. celebrity. Her first husband was Jon Hall, famous for South sea movies and set designs.

The two met on a radio show and were married just before World War II.

Hall and Langford purchased the property where the Outrigger resort was to be developed. The couple split up before the restaurant was built. Langford then married millionaire Ralph Evinrude of the boat motor fame and they constructed the Polynesian palace known as the Outrigger.

Francis Langford brought to this area of Jensen Beach many of her old friends like Bob Hope (who she traveled with during wartime entertainment shows all over the world.

The list goes on to all of the old-timers as they are referred to now. Jack Benny, Frank Sinatra, Peter Lawford, Jimmy Stewart, and many others you will see on the walls inside the now restaurant called The Dolphin Grill and Shrimp House.

Francis Langford continued to live in Jensen Beach and became a very renowned philanthropist supporting the local hospital, libraries, theaters, and all of the surrounding organizations that help the community. She still made herself visible to the public and would appear at dinner with her family.

It was on one of these special occasions at The Dolphin Grill and Shrimp House when I was dining with my wife to celebrate our anniversary in a private dining room, when the manager came to ask if we would mind sharing the room. Naturally, we accepted the company, for it was such a large room and they started moving table around. Then in marched about twelve people followed by a beautiful older lady with white shorts and a white blouse. She sat at the head of the table and smiled so graciously at everyone.

I immediately said to my wife, "I'll bet you breakfast tomorrow morning, that the lady is Francis Langford."

My wife said, "No, she is dressed only in shorts and a blouse. That can't be the famous lady." Those eggs and bacon we very sweet and I will always remember the special occasion.

The Dolphin Grill and Shrimp House is now owned by a restaurateur who remembers as a young lad dining with his parents at the Outrigger. He recalls how Francis Langford used to make such fuzz over all the young children who accompanied their parents. Never did he think he would now own the establishment. He does not use the resort dwellings, which I still remembered as being very nice. They set empty but for some storage and extra parking in the carports.

The dining is pleasant on the Indian River and can be enjoyed by eating inside and outside along the deck. Make sure to put it on your list of places to see in Martin County.

CHAPTER 29

FRONT LINE OF DEFENSE

It was June in 1984 when I completed my application for a Food Service Sanitarian for Palm Beach County Health Department. The interviewer was originally from Michigan as was I and he was quite sure I had met and even surpassed the requirements to be hired. Therefore, it was a very big surprise to us both when the application was returned from Tallahassee as unacceptable and I was astounded. The interviewer was very bothered by the results and immediately suggested I write to my State congressman to answer why a ex-military man with fourteen years in foodservice experience as well as a bachelors degree in business was not eligible for the position.

I immediately got a letter off to the Senator and a response was just two days later that I was to report to the Palm Beach County Health Department and begin training for the open position. It seems that someone up in the State Personnel office did not like Northerners coming down here to take their jobs.

The training was a lot of reading regulations and rules to follow. Then indoctrination to medical, dental, and eye-care benefits, as well as financial benefits for the position that boiled down to $7,000 per year job. Wow, what an adjustment from the $25,000 I had earned last year.

Completing the training I was assigned to an area in the City of West Palm Beach and the town of Palm Beach. I had a supervisor that was very good with young people and would always encourage his subordinates with pep talks about how we were the first line of defense for the protection of the public.

The program was quite comprehensive and that we were inspecting food service eateries, school kitchens, day cares, nursing homes, and elderly care facilities. We had a standing joke among all of the inspectors at the end of the day, (did you step on a child today?).

I stayed at the health department for just less than two years and took a month off to possibly return to Michigan. When I was not able to find any work in Michigan I returned and received my old job back. I had worked at the health department long enough to be promoted from a Health Specialist A to a Health Specialist B with a salary increase as well. I was very grateful to be accepted back and went right back to my old areas.

Shortly thereafter the Department of Business Regulations advertised an opening working for the Division of Hotels and Restaurants. I had heard about the opening from one of their inspectors that worked in

Palm Beach. She thought I would really like the position so I applied. At the same time an attractive German girl I had just trained at the health department heard about the same job and applied as well.

Immediately I set out to prepare a resume and bring it up to date. It was curious how the German girl and I began to compare notes and plan for the possible upcoming competition for the same job. She would come to my desk and see what I was working on and I would let her know that my resume was not quite as I wanted it to be. She would say that I had a good idea and then disappear.

Later that month I received a letter asking me to come to Ft. Lauderdale for an interview. It was quite exciting in that the German girl did not receive her letter. The next day she did and we were to be interviewed on the same day. We talked about traveling down to Ft. Lauderdale together but she preferred to travel alone or with her boyfriend.

So the day arrived and I made the drive down to the central part of the city. The office was located in an all glass Florida State Building just off I-95 and Broward Blvd. The parking lot was jammed but I found a place outside the parking area on a side street. It was on a grassy area where there were no parking meters. There were parking meters even in the main parking areas and a parking garage next to the main building.

The drive down to Ft. Lauderdale was quite stressful as I was used to the country or rural areas of Palm Beach County and Martin County. The busy traffic of a large city did not fit my life style that I had become accustomed to. The very large dark glass building was very impressive and the nerves began to come forth as I made my way to the main entrance.

A large sign on a chrome stand stating Division of Hotels and Restaurants, directed me to the 1st floor and to the left. I opened the eight- foot high double door and was greeted by a sharply dressed lady standing behind her desk with a stack of inspection forms that I recognized in her left hand.

A warm welcoming smile was on her face and she said, "You must be Steve Schultz. You're right on time, just 15 minutes before your interview".

I nodded with a yes and she directed me to take a seat on the chairs lined up to her right. She stated, "Lou Reif, our director will be with you in just a moment. He is in the middle of another interview and you are next".

Sitting there with great anticipation and nervousness I was interrupted several times by personnel passing. They would stop to introduce themselves and proceed to an office just to the right of the hallway leading down to the director's office. Later, I would learn the office was that of the district supervisor.

Finally, at 9:00 a.m. Mr. Reif's door opened and who should appear but my German friend from back at the Palm Beach health department. She was strikingly dressed in a silk dress with a half-calve length hem, glistening nylons that showed off her beautiful legs, and a brilliant smile, as she extended her hand and said, "Hello, Steve. Good luck"!

As I rose to shake her hand and smiled back at her, I was unaware that she got to the office before me and was scheduled to proceed me. That's when I heard a deep voice with much authority speak, "You must be Mr. Schultz. Follow me and have a seat in my office".

Lou Reif appeared dressed in suit pants, white shirt, and tie. His white hair was thinning but neatly combed to cover the balding spot on top. I immediately notice his wing-tipped shoes, which were brightly shined, as were mine, and he walked behind me.

While I was sliding into the first seat in front of his desk, Mr. Reif eased around to his large office chair on the other side of the desk. He reached for a file folder that I noticed held my resume. The first thing he said was "Did you have a safe trip down here and did you have any difficulty in finding a parking spot"?

"No, but I had to park on the grass along the side street where I noticed others had parked", I replied.

"That O.K., I'm glad to see you are resourceful. We will get you moved before 12 o'clock because that is when the police will start ticketing those cars", Mr. Reif added.

The interview started with Mr. Reif noticing that I was a veteran. He spoke to me about my service and why I got out of the Army after just three years. I explained my desire to use the GI Bill to get a college education and I also hoped to avoid being sent to Vietnam. I told him the timing was just right as Vietnam was almost over and I didn't want to reenlist anyway.

Mr. Reif explained that almost all of his inspectors were retired veterans and had the maturity to handle any problem in the field while doing the duty as health inspectors. They would be handling money for the State and approving establishments for licensure after the county inspectors had done their initial inspection. His inspectors would have the final approval after they also did an inspection.

Mr. Reif was really impressive the way he handled himself and explained the duties I would be required to perform. He also told me the area I would be responsible for and that I would be counted on to get the work done with very little supervision. The job required someone that could handle the task at hand working out of his own home, traveling a lot, and daily work results recorded and mailed to the district office daily. A state vehicle would be provided and records kept on its operation and maintenance.

I was very confident the job was something I could handle and tried to convey my experience in the past like the responsible positions I had held in the military as well as in the private food service industry. The completion of the interview was reached as Mr. Reif and I shook hands and he told me I would be notified of the results within the month.

I left the room feeling very good and thanked the secretary for her smile and courtesy. She said, "I hope to be seeing you soon".

I felt the same.

The trip back to Palm Beach County was a little less hectic because everyone was not trying to get to work. Still the Ft. Lauderdale traffic was three times busier than I was accustomed to. I stopped by the county health department to let my supervisor know that everything went well but I would have to wait to find out the final results. I stayed until quitting time to complete some paperwork and prepare for the next days schedule.

The German girl did not report back to work but on the following day we met in the office. She stated she didn't think her interview went well and she was not that thrilled over all the traveling that was required by the job. That made me hopeful but then I wasn't sure how many others had applied for the job. Thank goodness the month was almost over and I would hear something before the end of two weeks. I was anxious to say the least.

Finally, in the last week of the month, I had returned to the office to find a white business envelope on my desk from the Department of Business Regulation – Division of Hotels and Restaurants in the upper left had corner. My named appeared Stephen V. Schultz – Sanitarian, Palm Beach County Health Department, West Palm Beach, Florida as the addressee.

Nervously, I picked up the letter and then I noticed my supervisor, the director, and several of my fellow inspectors were gathered at the office doorway. It seemed everyone was as curious as me to the letters contents.

With a shaking finger I slid it between the envelope flap and pulled out the one page letter. The first thing I noticed was the signature of Lou Reif.

The text stated I was to report to the District 2 office by the first of the month and receive my state vehicle and start training for the position as a State of Florida inspector under the Department of Business Regulation and the Division of Hotels and Restaurants. I held the letter in my hand over my head and smiled with an exuberant "Yes"!

The group at the door awaiting my response all came forward to pat me on the back or shake my hand and wished me well. They all knew how much I was looking forward to the advancement.

My second trip down to Ft. Lauderdale was in a much better mood. I didn't mind the busy traffic or the waiting at traffic lights, or the difficulty in finding a parking place. This time I parked in the parking garage and was later able to provide a pass to leave. Arrangements were made to get a state vehicle assigned to me and would be delivered to my home by another inspector. The state license plate would allow me to park in front of the building without a problem.

Mr. Reif met me at the office door at 8:00 a.m. and it was the beginning of a long relationship where great respect for one another was nourished. We talked each and every time I came to the District office and on the phone as the job would dictate. I always held the utmost respect for this leader of mine and tried to exemplify his trust and faith he had bestowed on me.

The first month on the job was spent at the District office and I studied all the regulations pertaining to the position. At times it was very boring reading regulations but yet the understanding of the whole process of working with the industry, regulating the industry, and the goal of completing your job to a level of 100% was grasped. I was bound and determined not to let Lou Reif down.

The materials issued to a state inspector were much more than was available to a county inspector. Thermometers for food as well as high temperature thermometer for dishwasher machines, litmus papers for concentration of proper chemicals, flashlights, batteries, alcohol swabs for sanitizing thermometer stems, hand washing signs as well as signs for proper hand washing procedures, three compartment sink procedures, and finally the all important street cards and computer printout of accounts.

The street cards were complete with the names of the business, address, owner's names, address, and phone number. Each card was assigned its proper license number by county and number with its designation as an "R" for foodservice or "H" for lodging. The computer printouts were large sheets attached noting all the information that was on the street cards except the dates of inspections where listed under each. Foodservice establishments were to be inspected four times a year, Lodgings such as motels or hotels were to be inspected four times a year, and apartments were to be inspected at least two times a year. This all had to be completed 100% by the end of the year.

At the conclusion of the first month of studying the regulations at the district office, I was introduced to

James Gallagher. He was a crusty old inspector that had been with the department as long as Lou Reif. It was no accident that Jim, as I was instructed to call him, was assigned to train me. He lived next to the area I would eventually be responsible to inspect. Jim was very good at training inspectors and he really knew the job well. He insisted that I follow his rules and be prepared each day to accomplish the task before us.

Jim was very patient but very insistent that I follow his instructions. Every day was ended by recording the results of the inspections on the street cards, complete with date and violations. Then the report cards were filled out and attached to the daily reports that listed the inspections. This was all mailed to the district office before 5 p.m. each day. The inspection dates were also added to the computer printout sheets as well.

No day was complete until the next days schedule and inspection sheets were filled out with all the information except the violations that were to be recorded during the inspection. Each following day seemed so much easier and exciting as I was prepared and looked forward to a complete day keeping on schedule to reach that 100%.

The day finally arrived, as I was ready to be on my own but was always able to contact Jim if I had run into any problem. I really appreciated the time and patience Jim had taken to train me and I was so excited about being a well trained Florida State Hotels and Restaurants Inspector.

The first assigned area I became responsible for was the Town of Palm Beach, the East side of West

Palm Beach along Flagler Drive, and the area along the railroad tracks in West Palm Beach up to Riviera Beach. This was an area I had covered as a county employee and felt very comfortable with it.

The Town of Palm Beach had a lot of very high-end restaurants. I would dress in a sport coat and tie to make the owners and customers feel at ease while I was doing my job. I felt it paid off and I gained their respect as a professional and got the respect from everyone in the town. The police department and fire department worked with me, as I needed their assistance.

The job also required the inspection of lodgings, which included places like the Breakers Hotel, rental condos, and private homes open to rental apartments during the tourist season. I was to meet some very influential people but found them to be just as normal as anyone else.

The first few weeks were spent doing at least four restaurant or food service locations in the morning and then in the afternoon four lodgings were inspected. This pace would keep me up to completing the area assigned to me by the end of the year. Each month there would be an area meeting held by Jim Gallagher for all the inspectors from Palm Beach County and Martin County. We would usually meet at a centrally located restaurant in Palm Beach County. It was a surprise when I found us meeting at a Howard Johnson Restaurant that I used to manage when I was in my earlier career in mangement.

The department had to be satisfied with my work as I was selected to take over all of Martin County as well as the Town of Palm Beach. It did require me to increase the amount of inspections in the morning and afternoon. I also would complete a few extra each day. They were mostly the apartment buildings because it was an exterior inspection.

Now, I would come to understand how much I respected Lou Reif as a director and how seriously he worked with his inspectors to make sure the district completed its annual goal of 100%. We would occasionally have callback inspections to make sure violations were corrected. There was also a time when a licensee would be brought to a hearing that was held at the district office if violations were not corrected. All these events might put an inspector behind in reaching the 100% mark. But, Lou Reif would always keep track of each and every inspector's progress and you would receive a telephone call to let you know that additional work had to be done in order to stay on course of 100%.

The time when Lou Reif would make it a point to go out in the field and travel with the inspector really gave the inspector a feeling of complete respect. Mr. Reif would always let you know how much he appreciated you and the job you were doing. He also enjoyed getting out of the office and I always picked out the best location to have lunch with him. I knew he was a Cuban sandwich addict and I took him to a restaurant on the ocean that specialized in that cuisine. It also didn't hurt that the beach was full of bikini-clad sunbathers. His visit to

Martin County was completed with a lunch at Harry and the Natives in Hobe Sound. It was during this lunch that Mr. Reif expressed to me how much the department appreciated the work that was accomplished in the areas that I was responsible to inspect. They really acknowledged that no one had to call to get me to get out and work or had to check on me to see if I was working. He was so grateful that he told me that he looked forward to coming to work with me. I let him know that I looked forward to going to work for him every day.

Lou Reif had a comrade with the Department of Business Regulation. His name was Benny Hernandez and he was the hearing officer for the Division of Hotels and Restaurants. Mr. Hernandez was well respected by all of the inspectors. When a hearing was held to enforce non-compliance to violations sited by an inspector, Mr. Hernandez required the inspector and the property owner to be present. He would then listen to both sides of the incident and finally give his punishment or final decision on the case.

One particular case I was personally involved with brought an apartment owner all the way from Martin County to Ft. Lauderdale where Mr. Hernandez held his hearings in the district office. I rarely brought property owners to a hearing. I always felt it was my responsibility to work with the industry and get compliance in the field. Once communication was lost and no compliance was achieved, I would then call for a hearing. I was always at the bottom of the list for inspectors calling for hearings.

This particular case involved violations at several locations and the property owner was responsible for the corrections at each location. When he entered the hearing office he looked at Mr. Hernandez with disgust and started complaining about the distance he had to travel and he didn't have time for this. Mr. Hernandez sat behind his desk with the pile of inspection reports in front of him. He had a way a twirling his Knights of Columbus ring on his right hand and looked down at the thickness of the paperwork.

The property owner then made a very crucial statement that set the tone of the hearing. He stated, "I pay more property tax in Martin County than anyone else in the county"!

Mr. Hernandez finally raised his eyes to look directly at the property owner and stated, "Well, I'm glad to hear this. So, now I know you can afford these fines I am about to levee on your properties! Mr. Schultz, the inspector for these violations, do you have anything to ad"?

"No, sir. I just want the property owner to understand that I tried to handle this in the field but he would not even answer a phone call or meet me at the properties over this long length of time".

The property owner almost fell off his chair when the fines of almost $5,000.00 were imposed. He was given 30 days to correct the violations and pay the fines or they would double. Mr. Hernandez, twirled his ring again and reached across his desk to ask the property owner if there was any misunderstanding.

He then reached to shake my hand and congratulated me on a job well done.

The department had requested an inspector to go over to the West coast and work because the inspector there had a medical emergency. I volunteered and after about two months of working in the Ft. Myers area I returned to Martin County with a 19 foot fishing boat (a hole in the water to pour your money into). This was something I really didn't need but my son was taking a class in marine mechanics and I thought he could use the hands-on experience. Later I realized the only hands-on experience was his ability to push the throttle to full speed ahead and the boat had a short life.

But, on one of Mr. Reif's visits to Martin County he saw the boat and said that he had always dreamed of having a boat to fish from in his retirement. He really liked the boat but was shortly afterwards diagnosed with cancer. His health started to decline and retirement was planned.

I was always very proud of the fact the 100% goal was reached in every year that I worked for Lou Reif. Mr. Reif worked for the department even while fighting his cancer until his retirement. He also gave 100% right to the end of his job with the department. A very large retirement party was planned to take place on the top floor of a condominium in Ft. Lauderdale. Everyone was invited even the wives and many other dignitaries from Tallahassee arrived. The dinner, complete with

Cuban sandwiches, was wonderful and then there was the time for speeches and ceremonies. They asked me, as the youngest employed member of the organization, to speak first. 123

I started by telling everyone about the first interview with Lou Reif and how I was afraid that I would be passed over by the beautiful German girl. Then I expressed how much I respected and appreciated Lou as a boss and fellow worker. He was always there for you with his open door policy, his continued monitoring your progress, and his striving to get the entire district to complete their assigned duties by 100%. His loyalty to always have your back and ready to go the extra mile for you was greatly admired by all his workers.

Then I told them about his travels to Martin County and how he had his eye on an old boat in my yard. Lou said he wanted something like that to spend his retirement fishing. Unfortunately, Lou was not going to be able to do much fishing after his cancer. Anyway, I brought out of a bag a present gift-wrapped with a bow and all. He removed the covering and found a model fishing boat under glass. The boat had a Florida State flag flying from the bow; the sides were labeled with The Martha B. (Mrs. Reif's name), and across the back were labeled Department of Business Regulation – Division of Hotels and Restaurants.

I could tell Mr. Reif was touched and when he asked for the real one I told him that is all I could afford on an State inspectors salary. Everyone understood and applauded.

The dignitaries from Tallahassee followed with the usual plaque and extremely gracious words for Mr. Reif and how the Department depended on his skills and expertise in operating the office with sound practices and procedures.

Then the man we were all looking forward to approached the podium. Mr. Benny Hernandez strode to the front in his usual commanding manor. He looked out over the group and back to Mr. Reif. "Well, its been a long road, hasn't it Lou, old buddy". He continued to tell of their early days with the State of Florida when they both worked for the Department of Alcohol. They had to carry guns and baseball bats while running through the everglades looking for illegal stills. It was a time when prohibition was throughout the United States. This did not make Mrs. Reif very happy and when the Division of Hotels and Restaurants position was offered to Mr. Reif he had no arguments from his wife.

Benny Hernandez elected to still work as an enforcer and joined the department as their hearing officer. He told us how he and Lou had a hard time changing their ways, as they went into rooming houses, bars, and brought along baseball bats to get the attention of owners that didn't understand they were to be licensed. The size of these two guys was enough to scare anyone.

I reflect back to a time they both came to Bellglade with me on a particular case. Benny Hernandez said they had a little problem in a bar that had given the State a bad check and he wanted to collect it. To my surprise he went into the bar with a baseball bat and sure enough he had the cash in his hand when he came out.

Benny Hernandez kept us all laughing and astounded by his many stories of his best buddy Lou Reif. We were all saddened to know we would never have another boss like Lou or fellow employee like Benny. They were unique and very powerful and therefore respected by all.

The retirement party was the last happy time in the department as we were later to gather for Mr. Reif's funeral. The department would never be the same or as good as it was back then. Many changes were in store for the department and the division. I will not comment on the good or bad but I will just say it was never the same.

CHAPTER 30

WHERE SHOULD I EAT?

A health inspector when retired or still working is always asked, "Well, you should know best. Where should I eat? Which restaurant do you recommend"?

The answer I would give is for the cleanest and best run restaurant that I had inspected. It would sometimes be a private club or the smallest mom and pop operation. If they would ask for a particular cuisine I would then recommend the one that fit the above criteria of cleanliness and proper operational skills.

The question was recently asked of me for my recommendation on how to select a restaurant as a common customer without a referral. This is why I decided to add this chapter to my book on A Health Inspectors Memoirs.

A stranger to an establishment might first ask around for advice but if there were no recommendations I would suggest a person should use their common sense. Finding the location might be an alert if the place was located in a good area or a rundown area of town.

Next I would look at the parking situation. Is it accessible to the entrance of the establishment, does it have valet parking, or park on your own, with handicap parking provided if needed. Is the parking area well lit or maybe have a security guard or cameras. If there are parking meters will it cost more than the time you have to eat at the restaurant?

A quick drive by the establishment or a quick stop to look at the front of the restaurant will help to determine if you want to stay. If the front of the business is not well taken care of with clean windows, doors, sidewalks, or landscaping it might be a sure sign of how they care about the food and service they would prepare for you. A restaurant that keeps a fresh appearance up front will usually have a good welcoming approach for the public.

On your drive by it might be worth your while to observe the back of the restaurant. The dumpster location and the back door of the establishment. I can tell you that the inspector always looks there and will site the owner if it is not kept clean and the lids to the dumpsters are kept closed. It will be a sure sign that the back of the house (kitchen) would be in the same order as their outside storage area for their trash.

When you open the door, do you get a good smell from inside? Is the carpet or floor clean and not littered? Are the walls and surfaces inside the restaurant clean, dust free, and uncluttered? Look up and don't forget the lighting and ceiling to make sure it is not neglected with cobwebs, missing light bulbs, leaking ceiling tiles, dripping air conditioning, or lacking any kind of repair.

If you are asked to wait before you are seated, take the time to run to a restroom. A restaurant that takes care of their restroom facilities is usually another good sign of a well-run operation.

The restaurant that is serving shellfish is required to have a sign posted at the front of the restaurant by the hostess area or inside the entrance that proclaims this fact.

Buffet restaurants should be approached with a lot of caution. Hot foods are to be hot and cold foods cold. You will not be carrying a thermometer with you but common sense will tell you if the temperatures are present. You will want to make sure that a sneeze guard if protecting the foods served and that children are kept at a distance as their busy hands sometimes get out of control when not being watched by adults.

If there is a hostess that greets you, consider his or her manner. Is it polite and communicative with a positive attitude or abrupt and inattentive?

How is their appearance? My personal objections are sloppy clothing, dirty clothes, too much piercing, and unkempt hair.

If you feel this is the place you want to eat or if you still have a doubt, it is not out of the ordinary to ask to see their last health inspection report. This inspection report is required by law to be posted and available to the public for review. If they do not have it handy, then ask if it is possible to take a quick look inside their kitchen. This is not meant to allow you to do a thorough examination of every corner of the kitchen but to just make a quick observation of the appearance of a well-run establishment.

The staff should be clean, wearing clean outer garments, hats, and gloves when preparing ready to eat foods. Floors are to be uncluttered, clean to a standard to allow safe operation, and well-lit food preparation areas are all standard practice.

A quick look around the dining area to spot the table settings will tell you if the silverware is kept covered on the tables. They should be wrapped in a paper napkin or stored in a way that only the handles are exposed and the eating portion is covered by the folded cloth napkin. Some fine dining establishments will bring the silverware to the table after you are seated. Here you can observe the waiter or waitress to make sure they touch only the handle portions of the silverware. A thumb on a spoon is a thumb in your mouth.

Take the time to look for a busboy or waitress clearing a table or wiping down the table or seat you are about to sit on. The staff is required to use sanitized cloths that are dipped frequently into a sanitized station, like a pail or container. The sanitizer can be bleach water, quaternary ammonia, or iodine solution. These sanitizers are to be at a level that is inspected by the health inspector on each inspection.

Observe the waitress staff that picks up dirty dishes and does not stop to wash their hands before returning with another order for the next customer. This is a sign that they are not practicing good food handler procedures. The results are the customers are subjected to all the germs left by the previous customer.

Now that you are seated and all the above have been met lets not forget the menu. Is it clean when it is handed to you or do you see lots of spots, splashes, and stains? You can immediately bring this to the staff member's attention and request a clean one. If the staff member returns the menu to the holding place without cleaning it you may want to let the manager know or determine if you want to stay.

While on the subject of complaints or observations you might want to bring to the managements attention, try and approach it in a respectful way. Let them know that you really want to enjoy the experience of dining in their establishment but hope they can correct your concern as soon as possible.

Be sure to compliment the staff whenever possible and look for ways to make your dining experience an enjoyable adventure. A positive attitude can always overlook a slight mistake or slip but if one is determined to make the moment a real unpleasant situation it will make your return very dubious. Your fellow diners would appreciate your respect also if the problems can be settled with the management in a polite tone so as not to cause a scene or disrupt the atmosphere.

I cannot tell you how many times I have been dining with a fellow who was an expert on the mixture of a soft drink and there is no way the management or owner was going to satisfy his disagreement. It was very uncomfortable for everyone at our table and blown way out of proportion. I try not to dine with this individual very often, as it is a reoccurring problem.

The experience of managing restaurants myself was always rewarding when I heard from an unsatisfied customer and I was able to address the problem immediately. The customer was happy, I was happy, and I was sure to let them know how much I appreciated the comments. The restaurants I managed were always striving to satisfy the customer and our popularity would always be shown on the bottom line.

I always had a comment that I would use with the staff. A satisfied customer is the cheapest advertising we could ever purchase.

So, I hope this will help anyone looking for that restaurant for a good meal, with good service, with good quality, and will match the good price.

Gratuity should match the amount of your satisfaction and be sure to look the check over for any mistakes. Point it out to the server even if it is in your favor. Treat them like you would like to be treated. By the way the gratuity if added to the check automatically must be printed on the menu.

I hope I haven't forgot anything and I hope you have a good dining experience.

CHAPTER 31

MEMORIES OF THE PAST

The past is full of memories that will forever be in my mind. Most of them were pleasant experiences and very few were bad.

The pleasant memories are the ones that will last forever and I will always smile and feel very good. The bad ones are starting to fade as I grow older and it is good because life is getting shorter and I don't like to dwell on them a lot.

The best are the times that I would work out a problem with the operators of an establishment and eventually the problem was solved. The earliest problem was when I met Willie Mays, he said his name was, and the towel roll was lying on the floor covered with dirt and mud from the customer's shoes. We worked together to mount a new roll inside the old machine and I marked his violation as complied. He was so grateful and expressed his appreciation, as he had never had an inspector help him ever. I was pleased and left feeling that I had done a good job.

Then late in my career I was to undergo a certification and examination by one of the supervisors assigned to go with me on inspections and rate my performance. I happened to be assigned with the supervisor that was in charge of training for the district. We had never worked close together in the field and I felt we were both a bit nervous. As it turned out I had made a terrific impression on the supervisor for a correction of a violation involving the chemical concentration in a dish machine.

It seems a new dishwashing employee was instructed to open and attach new containers of soap, sanitizer, and rinse solutions to the dishwashing machine. It was a HOBART or a "one arm bandit" as we would like to call them while in the food service industry. Immediately upon testing the chlorine sanitizing level it was not registering anything on the litmus strip. I looked the containers over and promptly noticed the problem. The tubes leading to the containers under the machine were color coded so a mistake could not be made as the containers themselves had labels with the same color. The soap tube was in the rinse container, the sanitizer tube was in the soap container, and the rinse tube was in the sanitizer container. A quick switch of the tubes, coordinating the proper color matches and the problem was solved after a few cycles of the machine. I recommended to the owner to wash the machine thoroughly and check his employer after giving them a lesson on how to operate the machine correctly. Violation noted on the inspection report as corrected.

When we went to the car to sit inside and discuss the certification observations, the supervisor was shocked. How did you know all that stuff about dish machines and how to switch the tubes? I answered him by saying that all is not learned from reading books, attending lectures, and taking tests. Fourteen years experience working as a restaurant manager gives you a sound resource of knowledge. It was little effort to help them correct a problem that the owner later told me he would have had to call a service representative and that would have cost him at least $100.

The supervisor went back to the district office and was telling everyone what he had learned in the field today. I was fully certified for another few years and as it turned out was my last as I was ready to retire.

CHAPTER 32

DANGEROUS WORLD

When I first started to work in food service and also public lodging it seemed to be a farely safe environment. Except for a few first incidents in my life I was ready for a pretty safe and secure future.

The first job during my college years while working my way through school I had a job at night mopping the dining halls and kitchen. No danger, right! Just don't slip on the soapy wet floor or trip over the mop. But, both these hazards were met and conquered without injury.

The first job out of college was running an apartment complex with 200 units to rent, keep serviced, and repaired. The live bird that found its way into the bathroom exhaust fan vent scared the tenant and also scared me off the ladder when I had to remove the fan motor to release the intruder. The second most dangerous event was the evening the swimming pool was taken over by a bunch of nudist on an extremely hot summer night. All was going well until I told my wife to call the local police as I was going to go lock up the pool area and have them all corralled for the police to arrest them. The plan did not go so well.

I went to the swimming pool, I walked past all those lovely bodies, and proceeded to pour acid into the pool; warning them all to leave the water as soon as possible. I then went to the main gate and was locking a chain around it when the leader of the pack sucker punched me in the mouth. It was just then the local police helicopter landed and about the entire police force of the town we lived in arrived on the scene. It was just a swollen lip but I learned to let the proper authorities handle these kinds of situations in the future.

I later entered the world of food service, cooking, serving, and entertaining clientele. It was quite a surprise to be required to prepare chicken dinner family style for 400 people. I used the recipe provided by the previous cook. I marinated three 55 gallon food grade containers with chicken breasts, thighs, and wings that were kept in a walk-in cooler overnight. The marinade was salt brine and seasoned with a secret recipe. The next day was spent grilling all that chicken, making mashed potatoes, gravy, and corn on the cob. The dining hall was full of families arriving from all over the United States and greeted with their first meal of a full week of vacation at this American plan resort.

The final dinner was also prepared by me as the general manager of the resort and sent the guests off with a T-bone steak dinner complete with baked potatoes, carrots, and strawberry shortcake with ice cream for dessert.

Thursday night was kids night and grilled hamburgers and French fries was the main course. The kids loved the entire day as the waitresses and waiters were keeping them busy all day playing games. As soon as they finished dinner they ran outside the dining hall to the concrete picnic table behind the building. There they met the general manager and a wheelbarrow full of watermelons.

The staff purchased the watermelons from a local farmer. The melons had to be at least 20 inches long, red on the inside, and the soft ones were rejected. Thirteen of these juicy monsters could easily fill a full size wheelbarrow. The necessary tools for this event were paper plates and two very large sharp butcher knives.

The staff would line up the smallest kids first with their paper plates in hand and stand back a safe distance as I was handed the first melon to set on the wooden cutting board. First I waved the knife over my head then guided it over the length of the 20-inch long melon. Then with swift swoop the melon was cut in half and one half was set aside and the first half sitting in the middle of the cutting board. The red inside color lased with the shining black seeds made the children's eyes glisten and their mouths start to water.

Next there was the sound of the long sharp butcher knife slamming against the wooden cutting board through the watermelon, BAM, BAM, BAM, BAM, BAM, BAM, and BAM! Eight slices with each being two inches thick laid on the cutting board for each little tyke to pick up and put on their paper plate. "Now, don't forget to save your seeds for the seed spitting contest!" I would tell them. Then the next half melon was sent to the cutting board to meet the same fate as the first, BAM, BAM, BAM, BAM, BAM, BAM, BAM, and BAM! This was continued until all the little ones were served, then the teenagers, and finally the adults. This left just one melon in the wheelbarrow.

Behind the concrete picnic table and to the side was the shuffleboard court that served as our court for measuring the distance of the seeds that were spit. One week I could never forget, first up was the little princess in her finest dress and white-laced socks covered by her shiny black shoes. She looked very proper and was not sure how to go about spitting a watermelon seed. But, she puckered-up and let it fly.

She exclaimed, "Where did it go?"

The little red headed boy with the freckles, "Yelled, look down, it landed on your shoe!"

The youngest ones would get a ribbon for their efforts, the teenagers would get a plastic cup, and the adults got the last watermelon. All the bystanders and anyone still hungry for more watermelon shared it.

The position at this American Plan Resort only lasted one year as I found out what people said about never work for a relative. A relative who was an investment realtor bought the resort. He made a nice profit and gave us a pink slip after a successful year.

My next food service position was at the old drive-in restaurant that I used to frequent when I was a teenager driving a 57 Chevy. It seemed very strange managing the staff and the menu hadn't changed since I was a teenager. I was working on the night shift and it from wasn't very busy. The usual late night customers were coming from their work, bowlers from their night leagues, and the after hours bar crowd.

The menu was basically hamburger, fries, and fish and chips. The worst lesson learned that the staff could not be trusted as I caught several stealing food.

Later I decided we needed a vacation and my wife and I went down to Florida to visit my Mom. While visiting in Florida I answered an ad in the newspaper for a restaurant manager. The company was Howard Johnson and I left for Michigan with a promise to pay for my moving expenses, first months' rent, and a salary to start immediately upon my return to Florida.

The experience I learned from Howard Johnson would become very valuable to me in my later years working in food service. One thing I truly found out about myself was that I would never make a good grill cook. My morning cook was on his front porch passed out from a night at the dog track. It took me through breakfast before I could get away to bring him to work. The eggs I prepared were too runny and the pancakes were to burnt but for sure I lost a few customers that morning.

Security was the reason Howard Johnson hired me as I was placed in 11 different restaurants within 11 months. We found that many employees were stealing and gave the district director reasons to let them go. New employees were hired and it appeared to solve the problem. Many years after I left it was discovered that the district level employees did a lot of the stealing as they were skimming off the top on contracts for food purchased by the corporation.

When I was a manager of a Howard Johnson restaurant that had a bar, I learned how to inventory the amount of liquor on hand and the amount of liquor sold. Inventorying liquor was taking the bottles being used behind the bar, counting the full bottles displayed behind the bar, and counting the bottles still in the cases stored under the bar. Subtracting the liquor sold and the balance should be registered in the bar receipts for the day. The last location was found to come up short and when I questioned a few of the employees it was determined that my female bartender was supplying the local car salesmen.

It didn't take long with a little pressure from witnesses and figures to prove she had been stealing about four bottles a day. Her admission sent her out the door without criminal charges but the employment record would cause her to have a hard time finding another bartenders job in our town.

Howard Johnson treated me very well but the corporation that would pay all my moving expenses, plus tripling my salary, and providing me with an automobile got me to move back to Michigan.

The General Managers job at a 24-hour truck stop was a challenge I was ready to tackle. The doors never closed so there had to be many trusted employee working on all three shifts with managers supervision at all times. Fortunately for me a lot of these personnel were already in place but I did set up a program for promotion from within the ranks.

This didn't seem to bother two young upstarts I had hired to be grill cooks on the second shift. Their manager was the sister of the two brother owners of the truck stop whom I had great faith in her. But, she was distracted in the basemen long enough for the two banditos to escape with about 20,000 dollars worth of cash from the office safe.

The word was out for their arrest but only if the money was not returned. As soon as they discovered the amount meant grand larceny and time in jail, they gave up. A young friend of theirs came to me to ask for a job if she told me their identity. Need less to say they came to the office to give themselves in, with the cash. The girl got the job in our laundrymat.

The finale episode of danger was while trying to make an inspection in the most dangerous neighborhood as an inspector. I first thought that because the restaurant was located behind the local police station, it would be perfectly safe. Bad plan, as the local drug gang was making its weekly delivery at the same time. When I came out of the restaurant bullets started blazing all around me. I darted back in the restaurant and yelled I am not ready for this as I have only a week to retire. The police won the battle and I ran to my car to get out of there.

CHAPTER 33

A decade has passed since I retired and find myself looking around restaurants when I am dinning out for violations. It is impossible to forget and not enjoy a dining experience if the operator knowingly ignores the rules. Consequently, my wife and I do not go out much anymore. We do have our special places we look forward to and will accept invitations with our friends.

Since retirement, I first decided to donate one of my kidneys to my Sister in-law in Omaha, Nebraska. It didn't take long, only three days in the hospital and she was very healthy afterwards. The trip to Omaha was to fulfill a promise I made to myself to be a living organ donor. It was an experience I would urge others to pursue.

Next, I decided to start a hotel and restaurant-consulting firm that was known as SHRC. The letters stood for Schultz Hotel and Restaurant Consulting. My endeavor was to provide for restaurants to have a guide to help them get through inspections by being prepared for the inspectors.

I set the restaurants up with a white three-ring binder filled with plastic pocket pages.

The cover of the book had a photograph of the establishment and labeled with the name of the business. The back of the binder was labeled as RESTAURANT INSPECTIONS.

Opening the book you would find a table of contents with eight tabs. The first tab was the restaurant license and beverage license. The second tab would be the last inspection report. The third tab would have the Food Management Training Certification with the list of all the managers that had taken and passed the course. The fourth tab would have the list of Food Handlers Certification for the employees of the restaurant. The fifth tab would have the fire equipment report showing the hood system receiving its semi-annual inspection and the hood cleaning report. The sixth tab would have the restaurants Hand Washing Policy. The seventh tab was a special file for keeping important business cards, refrigeration, *A/C,* plumbing, and electrical contractors. The eighth tab was for the F.S. Chapter 509 and F.A.C. 61C-4 which regulated hotels and restaurants in the State of Florida.

I first called on restaurants in the areas where I was well known. The first client was very excited about receiving the book as a tool for operating their establishment and also to help train their managers. The picture on the cover of the book also brought about some pride in their restaurant. I never had a client refuse the book until the economy went bad and every restaurant establishment was operating on a very scaled back budget.

I will never forget the response I received when I introduced the book to a very well-known and successful operation. The owners reply was, "Finally, someone comes through my door with a brilliant idea"! To this day the restaurant is doing well and still using the idea.

The biggest surprise I get is when people approach me and tell me they remember me as their inspector. They usually tell me that I was the only inspector who came to them and was willing to answer any questions and sometimes I would leave them with a new lesson or idea that worked for them.

Many restaurant people would be disgusted with their inspector because the inspector was only there to give violations and send them to hearings for a fine. A lot of the inspectors did not have the experience in working in restaurants and knew only what was written in the regulations. I was one who would bend over backwards to teach the operator the right way to do things. I did not like taking them to a hearing as I felt that I was not doing my job property in training the restaurant or hotel operators.

When I retired, I tried to be a stand up comedian when I ran into one of the people I worked with in the industry. I would laugh and tell them I now answer to the name of Steve and not what you used to call me as an inspector. It was always nice and I was proud of the fact that most everyone I worked with or inspected their business had very nice things to say and I was grateful to have accomplished my goals with them.

Outside of a breakfast place I frequented there was a gentleman who drove in with a very old Cadillac that was in perfect condition. I had to tell him I admired the vehicle and he immediately told me he recognized me. He said I hadn't changed much in appearance. I questioned him if I had known him from another restaurant. He replied that he remembered me as his inspector in a coffee shop. He said I had been very stem with him over many violations in his place. But later he realized that I was always fair and only wanted to help him run a better place.

The one I remember the most and was so grateful for their response was an English couple that owned a very small motel on the Fort Myers beach on the West coast of Florida. I was assigned to that area for just a couple of months and really tried hard to satisfy my department by doing and extra nice job. They wrote a letter of appreciation to the department and expressed their surprise in how well I had not only performed the inspection but also made myself available to them. They had asked many questions about the rules and regulations and I was proud to go over many areas that they were not able to understand.

The letter went on to explain that they had been inspected many times but the inspector never took the time to answer any of their questions. I was grateful that they took the time to write the letter and it was placed in my file. Later I had to present the letter along with many others I had received to defend myself in a case against my department and the State of Florida.

My greatest pleasure is when I run into someone when I am doing our personal shopping and they will say, "I know you from somewhere but I can't remember your name". I will reply "Where you ever in the restaurant business?" The immediately, reply, "Oh, ya, you where our restaurant inspector. You were the best we ever had. What was your name again?"

I would thank them and reply" I go by Stephen Schultz now, not what you used to call me as your inspector."

Printed in the United States
by Baker & Taylor Publisher Services